"Jaffe adds to Brazil's well-established tradition of Jewish writing, which includes the likes of Clarice Lispector and Moacyr Scliar... *What Are the Blind Men Dreaming?* is an exquisite and original meditation on "the temptation, in some distant and inhospitable part of your memory, to have been in the survivor's place."
—BRUNA DANTAS LOBATO, *Ploughshares*

—

THIS IS JUST ANOTHER STORY *that will lose itself in the sea of survivors' stories, each one of them unique. There are no clear cut motives for telling this story. Both daughter's and mother's motives are uncertain, yet must be exposed: they are telling this story so that they might learn something, so that they might understand their memory and their forgetting, so that Mother's own micro-story might be inscribed onto the body of the world. These words can come to replace the memory she lost; not only because it is through them that it is told, but because these words can be used to anchor something whose natural tendency is to disappear. First of all, this book is an anchor for what Mother herself forgets. Secondly, for the daughter, this book is a token of what it is to try to be another person's memory, to be her mother's memory.*

Finally, this book is simply the daughter's attempt to come to know her mother better.

WHAT ARE THE BLIND MEN DREAMING?

—

Noemi Jaffe

TRANSLATED FROM
THE BRAZILIAN PORTUGUESE BY
JULIA SANCHES

&

FROM THE SERBIAN BY
ELLEN ELIAS-BURSAĆ

DEEP VELLUM PUBLISHING

DALLAS, TEXAS

Deep Vellum Publishing
3000 Commerce St., Dallas, Texas 75226
deepvellum.org · @deepvellum

Deep Vellum Publishing is a 501c3
nonprofit literary arts organization founded in 2013.

Work published with the support of the
Brazilian Ministry of Culture / National Library Foundation.
Obra publicada com o apoio do
Ministério da Cultura do Brasil / Fundação Biblioteca Nacional.

 MINISTÉRIO DA CULTURA
Fundação BIBLIOTECA NACIONAL

ISBN: 978-1-941920-36-7 (paperback) · 978-1-941920-37-4 (ebook)
Library of Congress Control Number: 2016950336

—

Cover design & typesetting by Anna Zylicz · annazylicz.com

Text set in Bembo, a typeface modeled on typefaces cut by Francesco Griffo
for Aldo Manuzio's printing of De Aetna in 1495 in Venice.

Distributed by Consortium Book Sales & Distribution.

Printed in the United States of America on acid-free paper.

Table of Contents

—

INTRODUCTION

Noemi Jaffe

In April of 1945, approximately a year after she was taken by the Nazis from her hometown, Senta, in what is now Serbia, and after she had been a prisoner in Auschwitz and Bergen-Belsen, my mother, Lili Jaffe (née Stern) was saved by the Red Cross and taken to Sweden. In Malmö, where she was quarantined along with her three cousins, who had been with her throughout it all, she wrote a war diary in which she tried to recreate those recent events that seemed to her most important: that morning in Senta when she, her brother, and her parents awaited the arrival of the Germans; the many cities she was taken through; her arrival in Auschwitz; her transfer to other camps and work places; and, finally, her liberation. But, beyond being an account of these tragic experiences of war, what I find memorable in this diary are the passages that recount the days after her liberation: the arrival of the Americans; how they were welcomed by the Swedes and the Danes; the enormous quantities of food; her rediscovery of femininity; her preoccupation with beauty; her new loves; her longing for her parents; the expectation of returning home and finally knowing who else in her family had survived.

I've decided to retain some of the particularities of my mother's writing in her diary in order to preserve the spontaneity and the intensity with which it was written. Her intention, in Sweden, had been to narrate these events not as if they were being written *a posteriori*—as they in reality were—but to give the sense that they

3

were being written as they were lived, which would have been impossible, since pens, pencils, and paper would have been unfathomable during the war. But, because this writing took place after the fact, mixing testimony and memory, it gave rise to variegated verbal tenses, dates that move confusingly backward and forward in time, and imprecisions. I chose to preserve this disorientation, precisely in order to be faithful to what my mother was living at the moment she decided to write.

She had never been in the habit of writing. And yet, she'd insisted in registering these recent occurrences, after her experience in the concentration camp, with impressive lyricism and aplomb. While writing this book, I asked her why she'd wanted to write the diary, to which she immediately responded: "So you could read it!"

I'd known about the existence of the diary throughout my adolescence; it existed then as a mystery, a treasure that I, somewhat unconsciously, didn't want to unveil. But later, as an adult, after being approached by a friend—a filmmaker who had become interested in my mother's story and in her diary—my sisters and I insisted that my mother translate it into Portuguese. After a few failed attempts to have it published, and after some short news coverage with my mother where she was treated like the "Brazilian Anne Frank," we temporarily gave up.

During a visit to Israel, where my sister lives, the two of them decided to take the diary to Yad Vashem, where they planned to donate it for conservation and consultation purposes. It so happens that the diary itself has an internal narrative: my father had fallen in love with my mother during their return to Serbia in 1945 and, before he left for Hungary, certain that they would never see

4

each other again, my mother offered him her diary as a reminder of their friendship.

In Hungary, my father filled the remaining pages of the diary with declarations of love and speculations on life and war. But, one year later, "as fate would have it" (as my mother would say), she found him in Hungary, where she had gone in search of her identity papers, which had gone missing in the former Yugoslavia. In the end, they were married and moved to Brazil with the diary in their suitcase.

The Serbian employees of Yad Vashem read about this romance in my mother's diary and were anxious to know what had happened with the relationship between the two young lovers. Had they been married? Did they see each other again? Certain that this diary stood out from all the other objects in the museum, they reached out to the Spielberg Foundation and insisted that a crew film my mother telling her story. When they heard that the diary's protagonists had gotten married, they celebrated ecstatically. Today that film, along with the diary, is cataloged in the museum whose goal is to collect the testimonies of all WWII survivors. In this book, I have opted not to publish the parts that were written by my father, as they serve more as an appendix to the diary.

In 2009, my daughter, Leda, and I went to Germany and then to Poland, ending our journey in Auschwitz, in the depths of a Polish winter. We wanted to see where my mother had been held prisoner, to collect information, and to feel what we hadn't been able to understand. We were searching for something that escaped us. Our reactions were practically opposites, as you'll see, but both notable and intense.

MY DIARY (1944-1945)

Lili Stern

TRANSLATED FROM THE SERBIAN-CROATIAN
HANDWRITTEN DIARY BY
ELLEN ELIAS-BURSAĆ

Senta, April 25, 1944 [*]

Everyone around me, with me, is full of sadness. Unfortunately, we know what lies ahead. Papa has been sitting on the ottoman all morning. He stares straight ahead and says nothing. From time to time he sighs deeply, glances over at us, and shuts his eyes. Mama comforts us. She is not one to believe in evil but she is readying things, packing up the rucksacks, baking cakes, and at moments, in secret so no one can see, she, too, sighs briefly. My brother and I watched them for a while, and like two little children we went outside and sobbed. They didn't tell us anything but we knew. We knew the Germans would be coming for us in the morning at eight, that they would be driving us from our home.

Senta, April 26

We got up early; everything was prepared. At eight a.m. sharp they arrived. There were seven of them. One of them sat at the table and wrote. A second inspected our things. A third issued the order: in five minutes we should be ready, that we should be bringing food for two weeks.

It's raining. We're together, our whole family, they herded us into the Jewish school where all of us Jews from Senta were assembled. When we arrived, two "German women" searched us to check if we had hidden any gold. By evening we had all been gathered. We spent the night on the floor.

---

[*] The diary dates are given here as they appear in the handwritten diary. There are inconsistencies, such as a June 31st and several August dates which repeat, but rather than guess at what was meant we have left them as we found them in the original.

Senta, 27 April

At nine in the morning they herded us out of the school as if we were animals. The rain kept falling, the mud is knee-deep, old women, little children, they cry, the blows from the Germans hurt them, they shout, drive us on, our foot gets stuck in the mud, they don't look to see whether the person is old or a child, they beat, hit us, "Filthy yids, faster!" In pain and anguish we arrived at the freight car. Sixty-five in the freight car, the whole freight car weeps. We didn't know where they are taking us. Papa is still silent, he watches us. Mama hugs us, gulps her tears, but she doesn't cry. All day we traveled, we never thought of food, when we sat down we fell asleep, sitting.

Segedin, 28 April

We arrived at eleven in the morning. With heavy packages on our backs, we walk three miles through town. It was horrible. The children stumble and cry. The old women stop and plead for help. All in vain. If they didn't walk, they were beaten. To make the walking easier we threw things away and so with grueling effort we arrived. They put us into a single room on straw. There were about sixty of us. They gave an order: we were to keep the room clean, rise at five-thirty in the morning and go to bed at ten at night, we should choose an elder who would see to everything. They wanted to choose Mama, but Mama wouldn't have it. We stayed a month here. We swallowed dust. For food we had whatever we'd brought with us from home.

Segedin, 19 May 1944

Unexpectedly, in the evening at midnight they herded us out of the school. It is dark, we can't see. Again noise—sobbing, we ask for light. Fortunately, we get it. We came out, outside we were met by carts which carried our things. At the station, we stood in one line where they handed out the packages and then back into the freight car. All night we traveled.

Baja, 20 May 1944

We arrived in the morning. They herded us to a furniture factory near the station. Since there were many of us, they divided us into two groups. Half stayed behind and the other half, us included, they escorted to a plain old pigsty, which we cleaned and brought in clean, cold sand. We spent nine days in that pigsty. Papa became very sick with a high fever. My grandmother also got a cold. She was frail. Mama kept her strength up but you could see the strain on her. She always had an eye on us and did what she could to ease things for us. Nothing hurt her; she didn't feel the ordeal for herself. She and Papa would have taken on twice as much if only they could have spared us from feeling anything awful.

Baja, 28 May 1944

Yesterday there were still Hungarians around. This morning I saw a German in our yard and afterward there were more and more. We were no longer scared; we braced ourselves for the evil. At nine we were all supposed to line up single file and the Germans counted and moved us. That same evening, we left our pigsty and walked to the station. There were some 70 of us in a single freight car with our packages that they tossed in after us. Papa and another man arranged them; one row around the perimeter and another down the middle, so that each person could sit in his own spot. We traveled for six days with no water and food. Papa has a constant fever but he keeps going strong, Mama soothes us, hugs us, my grandmother cries. Her back and her leg hurt and she can barely sit.

Auschwitz, 4 June 44

We arrived. They drive us out and immediately take our packages. They separated the men from the women. Papa and my brother were in one line, while the five of us are in another: grandmother, my four-year-old girl cousin, me, my eight-year-old boy cousin, and Mama. Our line is long. From afar, we hear a German shouting, "Right, left." When we were close and we saw they were separating us, Mama hid me under her coat (it was dark) in hopes that she'd be able to keep us from being separated. We reached the first German, he shunted us to the left. The second also looked us over and he sent us to the third German who was also there. He pulled me out and sent me to the right. There were a lot of us young girls, including my friend, Katica Blaier. Together we wept. She had arrived after me and said that my mother had shouted to look after me.

At midnight, we went into the camp. We walked a long way until we arrived at a bathing facility. We went in. Inside there were a lot of German men and women who took from us whatever we had left. We had to strip naked and go into another room. Women there cut our hair. I tried to run away to a different room, but the same fate awaited me there. I was really sad about my hair, but when

I thought of my parents I felt no other pain. Later, when they had already cut our hair, we washed in warm water, and from the water—all wet and out into the cold, where they handed dresses out to us. It was sad but still we laughed. One woman who was thirty-two was given a child's short smock. She took it back but they wouldn't exchange it for her. One was given only a skirt with no blouse and another, a blouse with no skirt. It was cold to stand there wet and naked until my turn came. I was given a long black dress. They told me I was fortunate. In front of the bathing facility, we stood again single file. It was dark. One in the morning. A little later, when my eyes grew accustomed to the dark, I saw men standing next to us. I looked for familiar faces and caught sight of Papa and my brother and they asked me about Mama. I was about to answer when the Germans came over and shooed me away. We don't see anything around us except fire and flames. It seemed as if we were moving closer and closer to the fire. We were afraid but we didn't cry. There were some among us who wailed and screamed. Them they took somewhere. I don't know where. We arrived at a wooden house that they called the "block." Into this "block" went a thousand of us. Inside it was also dark and there was only one loud barking voice: "Wherever you are, sit!" I felt the damp concrete. I didn't sit, I just crouched. In the morning, I think it was after three, they drove us outside. They showed us how we should stand and they read us the rules about how we were expected to behave: Rise at three every morning. Go in a line to the *"waschraum"* from the bathroom back here in a line, five to a row, stand quietly, which is called roll call. At five, a German comes who will count us. At six they give out black "coffee" and when we hear the bell, roll call is over. After the roll call, back into the "block." At three in the afternoon, there is another roll call and at six, supper is doled out. A hunk of bread, soup, and margarine with one spoon!

To stand from three to six was horrible for us, but the very moment we couldn't see a German we'd hug each other so we wouldn't be so frozen. It was the most awful for us before the sun came up when it was coldest. We could hardly wait for the hot black water (it was nothing like coffee). When they doled out the bread for supper, I didn't dare bite it. The bread looked like a plain old brick. And, in fact, it was made of wood dust. The first day I didn't eat anything, the second day the same, but later I had to, I was famished, and what I was given was too little. There were 30,000 of us (thirty "blocks" with 1,000 in each) in one camp with a camp just like this one right next to it. There were at least thirty, and there were more even farther away that we couldn't see. The camp was one kilometer long. At the end of the camp there was a [sentry] post, and the camp was fenced with electric wire. There were altogether eight crematoria, which were constantly burning and the flame was visible.

The fourth day (because I was looking for people I knew), I found cousins of mine, girls, and from that day forth we were always together (for a month my diary was not in my hand).

4 July 1944

Yesterday we came here to the "C" camp. Since I didn't write anything for a month, I will write about what happened. I went hungry a lot and suffered badly. Our block was dilapidated like all of them.

When it rained we were as wet as if we'd been outside. The beds—if I can call them that—were a simple slat of wood stacked one above another into three bunks. There were 12 of us on each bunk. It often happened that we fell down onto the other bed (I always wanted to be on the top bunk where there wasn't any dust and I felt [there was] more air). We slept like herrings. When the side we were lying on began to ache, we all had to turn over. That was when we most often fell off. Then, of course, the person we fell on cried out in pain, and the next day as punishment we wouldn't be given anything to eat. And so it went, each day the same. One day Alis brought a potato and a piece of cabbage, which was a joy. We divided it precisely into fours and ate it as if it were the most delectable thing. On July 1 at the end of roll call, in the afternoon, a man came with a red armband and they called him a *kapo*. He was the kitchen supervisor and a German. He selected the strongest women for the kitchen. All three of my cousins were chosen and I didn't dare join them. On June 30, a heavy rain had fallen during roll call. I was wearing a thin blouse at the time made of flimsy fabric and a black skirt. We had to stand still and didn't dare lift even a finger. When roll call was over, I wanted to brush myself off a little. As I looked around, I saw that I was no longer wearing the blouse, it had disintegrated in the rain. Since I couldn't stand there half-naked, I took the little scrap of blanket we had and with that I stood. I was very sorry to be separated from my cousins and they were too. I cried and thought about what to do. We decided. That day we didn't eat, we sold our food and bought me a dress. We thought I'd be able to join them in line the next day, but since there was a precise count of forty-five, I was left to my fate. The next morning before we went out for the roll call, the elder of the block announced that if someone does not have a decent dress, she should take the blanket and stand next to the line where the girls for the kitchen were standing. At that moment I decided I, too, would take my blanket and stand with them. There were many of us standing with our blankets. I was at the end and at a moment when no one was looking I threw down my blanket and moved over to the line with my cousins. It worked. A little later they came to count us. As I already wrote, there were supposed to be forty-five, but now there were forty-six. I was afraid but I tried to hide it so nobody noticed. The German woman was very angry. She shouted: "If the one who was not selected does not step forward, everyone will leave here and go to the punishment sector." I did not speak up. I was ready for the worst. The angry German woman began selecting again. When she reached us, without a word she placed my cousins among the good ones and then stood in front of me. (Everyone thought I was a child, as I was petite and without my hair I looked no older than fifteen). "I selected you yesterday?" "Yes, please." "But you are still small, you don't know how to cook." "I do know how. I am not young. I have three cousins here and I want to be with them." She was mean but she joked with me, came to like me, let me stay and she threw out five others. Off we went. We were given new dresses. They gave me a really nice dress. Now I was no longer scared. I always stood right up front.

6 July 44

It is two days now that I have been in the kitchen. It is tough for us to get up at three in the morning and go to work straight away cleaning potatoes, cabbage, turnips, until midnight or whenever we're done. Yesterday was awful. We were told to clean 600 pounds of potatoes and 400 pounds of cabbages. All of this would have been done by six in the evening, but almost all day we had an assignment. To take down from the truck and lug into the storage room, first, 300-pound sacks of flour and then the same amount of sugar. Hardest of all was the salt in paper sacks, each of us carrying a hundred-pound sack. Afterward, the bread. Here we formed a chain and passed it from hand to hand.

When we'd finished we were bone-tired, and the most horrible thing was we wouldn't have time to finish prepping the food but we had to, so we worked all night until the next morning at eleven. I couldn't lift my arms. Groggy and exhausted at eleven p.m. we went to the block. This block was gold compared to the others. We had blankets, two per person, and they were of pure wool, and on the bed there were [only] six of us, lovely. For food, sweet black coffee and all the rest as much as we wanted. We were glad. If only the job hadn't been so grueling.

2 August 44

Almost a month has passed since I started in the kitchen. I am already used to the work and we have as much to eat as we need. But that's not enough for us. We have so many friends and relatives who are starving. The four of us can't watch this. Hajnal is in the storeroom with the margarine and sugar. She brings them out to us and we pass them on. It was very dangerous to organize stealing [because] when the German notices someone, woe to her. Yet we did it anyway. Since our friends weren't in our camp, I had to pass it over across the electric wire. This was very dangerous and I was the only one who dared. First it was the German, so he didn't notice because he shoots immediately. Second, it was that my hand mustn't brush the wire because that, too, means death. But it didn't hurt me, I wasn't scared of death because I'd understood everything with a cool head. Every day it went like that. 'Til I got in trouble.

The day before yesterday, Hajnal brought out margarine again. About a gram. Alis hid it right away among the cabbages, meaning to take it out in the evening before we went home. However, one girl asked Alis to give her a little margarine because she had nothing, and she wasn't feeling well so she couldn't chew the dry bread. I heard that and afterward they sent me to the end of the camp so I wasn't in the kitchen (they told me what happened next). Alis [was] like all of us. If we had something we couldn't say we wouldn't give it. Alis told the girl, "Keep watch so no one sees me while I take it out." While Alis was taking out the margarine, the German woman came and saw Alis. "What are you doing here?" she, frightened, says: "I am taking out a little margarine." "And where are you from?" "We are four sisters and we haven't been feeling well so we pooled our portions together." "You dare to say this to me?!" Then she slapped Alis. "Show me your sisters." I wasn't there so instead of me our friend spoke up. "So here you are. You'll kneel here in front of the kitchen until roll call—in an hour.

If you don't admit by then which one of you stole the margarine, I will throw all four of you into the crematorium. Alis didn't say it was Hajnal, and the others also didn't say. They kept silent. For me, while they were kneeling, I am on my way back. In the morning they told me what happened. I didn't even think about what I was doing, but ran straight to tell the German woman that it was my fault (even though I didn't know what this was about). When the other girls saw what I was up to, they grabbed me. They didn't want to let me go because they knew this was death, but I was stronger than they were. The time for roll call was near and I had to hurry. Why should four of them be killed when the Germans would be satisfied with one, and I was not afraid of death. I went in. I knocked on the door. Inside the German woman was with a German man. "Why did you come? What do you want?" I didn't know what to answer for a moment, I cried, and through my sobs I said, "Let my cousins go, they're not guilty, I stole the margarine." At that she jumped up, came over, and slapped me. "So you admit this just like that? Where did you take it from? Do you realize what you'll get now?" "Sorry, I know, I saw it on the table and I took it. I never will again." "No, I will show you what you'll get, you'll never see the sun again, mark my words!" I tried to plead for mercy but she wouldn't relent. At that point the German asks me: "How old are you?" (Of course I said a year less, "Sixteen.") "Sixteen? And you still don't know this must not be taken?" (He looks over at the German woman and whispers to her in a low voice) "Don't be so strict—you can see she's still young." At this the German woman fumed: "What? You're defending her? I'm off to the camp officer and he'll give her hers."

She left. Meanwhile, he took me out, over to a heap of rocks where he ordered me to kneel and hold over my head this huge stone I couldn't even lift. I picked up the stone but had to put it back down. I couldn't hoist it up. The German watched me struggle and said: "Be careful, if you aren't strong, the German woman will come and you know what to expect then?!" With huge effort I lifted the stone up to my head but I couldn't hold it and the stone dropped onto my head. Then I thought I'd faint, but I was strong. I was in terrible pain, the whole camp was standing at roll call, my cousins too, and my tears were dropping like rain from my eyes. Not out of remorse for taking it upon myself but from the pain. I knelt that way for two hours until the German came and someone [said]: "Get up, off to the kitchen with you, keep working!!" I put the stone down and wanted to stand. The sharp rock on which I'd been kneeling had made my knee hurt so badly that I fell. I heard the voice of the German again, I wanted to stand but didn't know [how]. I sat and after ten minutes hobbled into the kitchen where I fainted. My sisters cried, gave me cold compresses, and comforted me until I began to feel better.

Yesterday, further: No longer did we dare to even think of stealing something, but those who hadn't yet gotten into trouble were not afraid. They stole meat. The German woman noticed and since again she didn't know who'd done the stealing, she announced that the whole kitchen would have to perform a "sport" gymnastics drill. All forty-five of us stood outside. First, run three times across the yard holding a stone over your head, afterward hop across like a frog, and, finally, crawl three times around the yard on your knees.

Since the German woman was alone, it was easier because while she was looking ahead, we behind her only pretended to run, and vice versa. So it was going fine until she spotted me. When she did see me it was terrible. "Aha, so that's you, is it? Yesterday you stole margarine and today, the meat," and she began beating me. She broke three canes over my back: one on my head, the second on my back, the third over my chest. But that was not enough. She kept following me and didn't look at the others. They walked around, but she didn't care about them anymore. The five of us got it bad because we were together. One of us had her leg amputated, a second was operated on, a third as well, and I had a gash all the way to the bone, which I did what I could to treat on my own.

1 September 44

I had a lot of pain in my leg. Most terrible was that I began working already the next day. The first day I thought surely I'd never again "organize" anything but I couldn't hold out for long. Those to whom I had been carrying [food] until then were hungry and I had to, I couldn't keep myself from carrying [food] to them. One day I went through the camp and looked over into the men's camp that was next to ours. I was searching for people I knew, as always. Soon I heard there were new men who had just arrived in the last block. How I shouted. I inquired about Papa and my brother by name. A skinny man came out of the block who told me he'd been with Papa at the mine factory. When he came closer I was amazed because I knew him from Petrovo Selo Kaštiber. He recognized me, too, and was overjoyed. I asked him to tell me about Papa and he said, "We worked together, he looked good, he had enough to eat and besides they were given cigarettes and since I don't smoke I gave him mine." I asked him why he'd come back. "Because I am ill, I have malaria and besides I am too thin, I am thirty-two years old. I know they'll take me to the crematorium."

That same day I brought him a package. I'd obtained quinine, sugar, and bread. I managed to hand this over to him. And so I carried [food] to him every day. One day, five days ago it was, I got quinine for him and with a package of food I threw it over the wire. He thanked me and I told him, "Go, run, so no one notices you." He leaned over to pick it up and at that moment a German man appeared in their camp and the German woman showed up in ours as well. I noticed sooner than he and quickly slipped in among the other girls, and my heart was pounding in my throat when I looked at my wounded leg. Then I looked in his direction as well and my heart ached when I saw the German was beating him horribly. He threw him onto the ground and beat him until he fainted. The German took the package but luckily the quinine was already in his pocket. The next day the poor man couldn't get up, but by the third day I was carrying [food] to him again.

He succeeded in putting on ten pounds in three weeks and recovered from malaria. He was so grateful to me that he kept saying he owed his life to me.

30 September 44

Cold days have set in. The climate here is far colder than it is where we are from. We had good clothing, warm sweaters, and good shoes because we paid for them with food. I'm still having trouble with my leg and I can't wear socks. The sock kept sticking to the wound. It's difficult for me to write about what happened to me five days ago but as I have begun, I will write about it all. Next to us is the "C" camp where we stayed before they selected us for this place two months [ago]. In that camp were only those who were not working, while in ours were only those who were working. Each year in September there is a selection process for the camp where the non-workers are. How they took living women by cart and truck to the crematorium, and all of it could be seen. It was raining. The women were sitting in the cart and then men were pulling them to the crematorium. Whoever was a little stronger tried to run away and the German was constantly shooting. From early morning until night there was constantly moaning. We heard the shooting. I did not want to leave the kitchen. We cried. When I did leave (because I had to) all I could see was flame around me. This lasted for three whole days. During that time, it was "*blocksperren*," shutdown, which meant that no one could go out. I didn't eat then. I couldn't even think of eating. We were waiting for our turn to come one day.

15 October 44

The selection process is over. Since there are fewer people in the camp, there are too many of us in the kitchen and they told us only half could stay. We went out to roll call and half were sent off on a transport. We still stayed behind.

27 October 44

Even now there are too many of us. The transports are leaving the camp every day. Surely the Russians are getting close and that's why it is so urgent for them to empty out the camp. They also selected us with others in the camp to send away. At three in the afternoon we left our camp. We went to the "F" camp and stood in a row until midnight as if it were roll call and this for us was the worst of all up until then. We were each crying. We didn't know what they'd do with us. We were out in front of the crematorium. At about seven it is already dark. The crematorium burns and we see the flame blazing high out of the chimney. Every five minutes it subsides and then blazes again. After midnight we came into a block where there was a naked selection. "Raise your right arm and hold up your dress with your right hand," that was the order. My heart was pounding so loud I could hear it, that's how frightened I was. My leg is bandaged. I still have the wound from the "sport" [drill]. Right in front of me I see how the doctor selects to the left those who are just a little [illegible]. I was certain that with my leg I would also be going to the left. My turn came. I was quite scared. I held my dress so close to my body, clutching it in my right hand out of fear, which they found suspicious. The doctor grabbed me and held my right arm and looked me over. He thought I had some sort of wound on my upper body and that I was hiding it by holding my dress so tightly. But I was thinking I'd hold the dress close to hide my leg. When he saw I had nothing on my upper body he didn't even look at my leg and let me go. A miracle, everyone was amazed, I didn't dare hold on to my happiness because I don't know what yet awaits.

From that block we went into a bathing area where we were issued clothes. Mid-winter: a thin dress, a light coat, the shoes we had on with no socks. Since we had come from the kitchen we had food and we bought dresses, sweaters, socks with the food so we hadn't been so cold. We spent the night in a block.

28 October 44

Early in the morning we go to the wagon. Each person receives a whole loaf of bread weighing two pounds, a quarter pound of margarine, and a quarter pound of salami. Sixty-five of us to a wagon. We had room to sit and food to eat.

Belsen, 1 November

We arrived. We left the wagon and walked to the camp. Our feet ached from the walking. A long trek. We had already walked six miles when we hear shooting in the distance. The closer we come to the camp we hear it more and more clearly. Immediately we thought the worst as always and that was hardly surprising. The camp was fenced with barbed, but not electrified, wire. Inside the camp there were no blocks, just tents like there used to be for tourists but in the summer, not the winter. We were each given a dish, a towel, and a blanket. In the tent there were three bunks, but there were two of us sleeping on each. In the morning we had to come out for roll call at eight o'clock, where we received food. There was no bathroom, outside there was water trickling a little in droplets. There also was no toilet, just a pit with a board spanning it and pointing to the pit was a sign with the word "latrine."

13 November

We've been in this tent for thirteen days. It is extremely cold, especially when there is wind or rain. Last night there was heavy rain and after the rain, there were winds blowing that brought down the tents, ours only halfway, luckily. Above our heads there was enough still up that we didn't feel the rain and wind quite as much. In the morning when we came out we had something to see. Only three tents were left in a state similar to ours, the others were all downed. The people who were in them were chilled to the bone, freezing, in miserable condition, huddling together. After roll call we waited for the German.

He brought us to a different camp. In this camp there were nice masonry blocks with bathrooms and in the block there were beds where we also slept by twos. My partner was always Alis.

Cold, rainy days followed. The rain is constantly falling, outside there is such deep mud. We were fearful when we thought of roll call. But fate is not so harsh. They informed us we will be having roll call only once a week and it will be in the afternoon.

18 November 44

We spend all day in bed. We have enough to eat. They chose Hajnal to be the "*štubdinista*," as they call the helper, and this is good news, she gets more to eat. The food is reasonably good, in the morning there is coffee or tea, at noon soup with meat and in the evening, a chunk of bread with soup three times a week. When there is no soup then something different comes with the bread:

margarine or wurst. So that the time would pass more pleasantly and quickly, among us there was an older woman from B. Pest [Budapest] who organized a little group of artists. Among them, Alis chose to sing, and as for me, because she'd heard me recite she asked me to join them, too.

Every day in the afternoon there was a little fun, humor, singing, and reciting. I was given a really nice black dress and, aside from that, Alis and I had a double portion of food.

1 December 1944

We were very satisfied in this camp. We weren't required to work. We rested. Today we heard some news about political goings on. The Russians are in Auschwitz, and the Germans and the others who are still there are on their way to Bergen-Belsen. Of course we were not overjoyed because we knew there were too many of us and we were afraid of the Germans from Auschwitz. Furthermore, we also discussed how there might be a crematorium built here.

No longer were we in the mood for fun.

10 December

Today we came out for roll call early in the morning. We were selected for a transport.

13 December 44

They told us to get ready. Each of us went to our blocks and the camp *kapo*. Gizika was the most forlorn among us. She was dismayed that we were leaving here; Hajnal was, too. We tried to hide but it was in vain, we had to take our place among the others.

We are taking the same road along which we came to the freight car. They loaded 80 of us with no food or drink.

Braunschweig, 15 December

We arrived. The whole city is in ruins. At the moment we arrive we hear an alarm. The Germans, the local people, run; we are also urged to hurry. We were not afraid of the siren because we were not afraid of death, just of agony. We filed through the city and stopped in front of a ruined building and a little later we went inside. There was a vast stable in there where parade horses had been kept. The hay was already soiled, it was airless—"our new home." As it was already evening by then, we lay down in the straw and spent the night there.

20 December

Every morning at six we rise. Outdoors we stand in roll call, morning and evening. Outdoors it is snowing and very cold. At seven roll call was over and today we went into town in a line. In the middle of town they gave us shovels. Each of us has a shovel and with the shovel we continue walking. We entered a street where all we saw were houses in ruins. We were ordered to clear away the rubble from the pavement. Our hands were frozen and we were only allowed to light a fire after eight in the evening. Today it's eight degrees out. This was unbearable. When the German wasn't watching, we stopped working and puffed into our hands.

With misery and anguish we worked until two o'clock, and at two-thirty we made our way back. We returned the shovels. By five we had arrived. Here they counted us and as soon as we came in, we were given dinner.

15 January 45

The days passed, one much like the next. We wept from the pain and the cold. The straw on which we were lying could no longer be called straw. When we came back from working with muddy shoes, we walked on the straw and on it we also slept. There were so many lice that the straw squirmed. We had only one thin blanket to cover the five of us. Some slept in the dress in which they worked, but the four of us undressed.

5 February 45

Today we rested. We ate, we were given only a small amount, but that is enough when we aren't working. We keep after the older people, asking how it goes and what they do, and they keep saying, "You'll see."

Today we got up like every day at 3:00 a.m. The only thing making it more bearable is that we stand in the "hall" not outside. At about four we were given hot coffee and today they didn't send us back into the block in a line. Instead, single file, we went outdoors. Outdoors is freezing, snow. We didn't know where they were taking us. We didn't go far, about 600 feet. We stopped and entered a wooden…what can I call it? From the outside it looked like a hunter's lodge made of wood.

Inside there was nothing but an elevator shaft. We filed in five at a time. The elevator took us down below the ground 600 feet. The elevator stopped, we stepped out. A tunnel, two miles long, the walls of which were made of salt about six feet high. Anyone who was a little taller had to duck. It was about five feet wide and a railroad track ran through it along which they carried, or people pushed, little wagons with salt. We had limited air but there was enough light. This street was called "Hitler Street." We reached a second elevator. This elevator took us down another 900 feet. Again we got out. Before us was a similar tunnel but darker, so much so that there were some places where there was no light at all. A German carried a lamp and urged us on faster or they'd beat us. I can no longer feel my legs. We are walking more than four miles, I can't feel my legs, each of us is moaning; we still are not at the end and there is still far to go, as the people tell us who walk by. This is unbearable. After eight miles we arrived at a place where there were stairs going up steeply in front of us, straight up for about five stories. It was impossible. We went up a little ways, but we couldn't do it. Back down we came. We were already exhausted as it was. The German took mercy on us. We went up by elevator. When we stepped out from the elevator, we entered a spacious marvelous factory. Clean and vast. Electrical equipment and three women were at each table. A German woman and two of us. An airplane factory, but we were making only small interior parts. Our work was of no consequence. They didn't dare give us any tools because they were afraid. Just painting, and insignificant things like that. We rested. We were given lunch on site. Pretty good, carrot soup. If only the trek to get there were not so far.

5 March 45

For more than a month we worked there. We had already gotten used to the trek, so it almost didn't seem so far for us to walk. Along the way we were ordered by the German to sing. My leg was swollen—and not only mine, the others, too—because of the air in the mine. Almost half of us are having trouble with our legs. Unexpectedly on Sunday, it was nice weather, we were lined up for roll call outside. The Russians are ten miles away. It was so urgent to get ready to travel, not only for us but for the Germans, that they didn't have time to pack up any food.

28 March 45

Without food or drink. One hundred twenty in a single freight car. We couldn't budge. We managed somehow for the first night and first day. But it was rough on those—terrible really—who had no space. We were all so emaciated at that point, skeletons, barely able to sit upright.

1 April 45

We are still in the freight car with no food. But there are not 120 of us now because every day five or six died. The Germans come with the men from the camp and ask how many dead, "Only five?" We got to the point that we could no longer stand. I had tied up in a rag a little crumb of bread the size of a fingernail to insert in the wound because that is how I was treating it. I put it in my mouth, I meant to take it out and put it on the leg but I swallowed it. Horrible. The wound was all green. It ached something awful.

5 April 1945

We are not dead and we're not alive. Ninety are left of the 120. We're thirty miles from [Bendorf], near Hamburg, but we have no connection to travel on with. Airplanes fly constantly overhead. The men console us that liberation is near, but we don't believe them. I am finding it difficult to speak at that point. We ask the German not to torment us any longer. We do not want to live any more. This is killing us. As consolation he says: "We, too, are starving. Liberation is near. Try holding on just a little longer." We are in a forest. We know we can hold on for only one more day without eating. For six days we have eaten nothing. We plead with the German, crying, to kill us. "OK, if that is what you want. I can't watch you suffer. This afternoon at three, I'll grant your wish." We stopped. Typically there were fifty of us to a group. It was around noon. We sat down and awaited our death patiently. At exactly five p.m., the Germans are ready, we stand calmly and wait for the camp *führer*. He arrives immediately after five, beaming with cheer: "You are saved. At midnight, two truckloads of bread will arrive." The Germans are so relieved, they, too, are famished. They put down the guns and we went back to the freight car. Midnight passed and there was no bread. We moaned, but our voices were not loud. They couldn't be heard at any distance.

6 April

In the wagon. The ones who are left are the ones who haven't died or are not comatose. It is like I am drunk. I can't see, but I feel as if I am foaming at the mouth. At noon the trucks with bread arrived. The Germans themselves slice and distribute the bread. Each of us receives a pound of bread with margarine.

The bread was brought from Sweden. Again we had a little strength. We ate only a little because we held onto it and kept it for the rest of the days. In the evening we traveled on farther.

10 April

It is raining. We came out of the freight car. We'd arrived at [Ohsen]. The camp is not far from the station, but I was completely drenched by the time we arrived. The patients helped us down and then into the block. It was warm, there was heating. We were given food and allowed to rest. Alis and Hajnal went off to the kitchen so we were given a little more. For my leg I received medicine.

20 April

We're doing pretty well here. We have opportunities to keep ourselves clean because there is a bathroom. We don't have to work, we are able to rest.

25 April

After roll call, which was held twice each week, we didn't go back to the block, but to the station.

In front of the station we stood. We waited not for freight cars, but for an electric train that could carry sixty of us. Every hour it came back. For the first time I feel as if I am like other people. In this one I can sit on cushions on the seat. We arrive in Hamburg at five. The camp was also close to the station. At the camp, each person was given a bowl of red beet soup. We ate our fill. At the block there were many of us again on each bed, depending on how lucky someone was. There were eight of us, we were lucky.

Hamburg, 28 April

The rain has been falling hard for two days now. We have a German woman who beats us and we are very afraid of her. We hear in secret that they are close to Hamburg, that we will soon go home. We are afraid to think again of the worst hunger.

29 April

The German woman came into the block and chased us out. The rain is still falling. In single file we walk out of the camp. By the gate we see a German soldier with the Red Cross. We are in front of the freight cars. Only closed freight cars. Each person is given two pounds of bread and twenty-five of us are loaded into one freight car. There is straw in the freight car and in front of the freight cars is the *Wehrmacht* with the SS. We don't know what this might mean. We didn't dare contemplate anything good. I wanted to eat, but my cousins were afraid, especially Gizika who kept saying, "Children, let's guard our bread because who knows how long we won't have any."

Padborg, 1 May

We crossed the German border. We are in Denmark. The German jumps off the freight car and shouts, "Hitler is dead, the war is over." Danish nurses in white aprons from the Red Cross come and bring us out of the freight car. They offer us cakes; we no longer so much as look at our dark, dry bread. They cast flowers around us and carry us to a vehicle, fifty at a time. We arrive at a farm. Here they gave a speech for us. We mustn't be angry at spending this night on straw, but we must know we are so filthy and flea-bitten so until we get clean, we will be on the straw. Each pair of us was given a fine English warm blanket to share. Since it was already dark we weren't given dinner, so we went to bed.

2 May

At about eight, we lined up for breakfast. They told us we would have breakfast from 8:00 to 10:00, lunch from 11:00 to 2:00, a snack at 4:00 and dinner at 7:00.

It did not turn out the way that they were thinking. For breakfast we sat at a white table. First they served semolina cooked with milk, white bread and butter, later cocoa and a milk roll, two pieces of dark bread with salami, and as many cakes as we wanted.

We left the breakfast [room] through one door and by another door back in we went so that they, of course, didn't notice us. Three times I ate breakfast and still I wasn't full, and not just me. Each of us did the same. It's already noon and we still weren't finished with breakfast, so, furious, they closed the hall.

We came for lunch at two o'clock, but now they paid closer attention to be sure we weren't coming through twice. We sat at the same table. A fork, knife, spoon, all of silver. A nurse served the meal to each of us. First soup, then spinach with white bread and an egg, but a full plate, then compote, cocoa, cake, again as much as we wanted. They were surprised at how much we were able to eat. After lunch we were still hungry. Yogurt—they stored it in barrels for pigs. We began drinking it greedily. I didn't stop and neither did my cousins. Then we sat down on the ground, scrounged for firewood and potatoes, and we roasted the potatoes. And so we, sooty, grimy, ate a lot. We were all filthy. The Danish laughed at us. Painters came to paint us eating and how we were dressed.

2 May

In the afternoon we entered into the same car that had brought us there. At the station a second-class train car waited and we got on. Leather seats, pristine. In the train, a Red Cross nurse gave each of us another package. In the package: two slices of white bread with butter and cheese, two slices of dark bread with an egg and ham, with a cup of cocoa and a bar of chocolate.

The Danes got off at the station. They bedecked the train with flowers. They threw in sugar, chocolate, cakes, and whatever anyone had.

Along the way Danes were cheering, they shouted "Cheers" to me. We are traveling for quite a long time. By us passed trains carrying Germans, the nurse says these Germans are coming from Sweden, we are trading places with them.

Copenhagen, 3 May

At eight in the morning, we arrived in Copenhagen. The train stopped at the dock. We were already greeted by a huge ship, three stories tall. When we got off the train each person received a quart of yogurt which we immediately drank, and pastries. Then we boarded the ship. On the ship, single file, fifty of us entered the restaurant. Here we sat at tables for four.

Waiters came over with the menu, "What would you like?" We were speechless. The nurse noticed this and she ordered for us. Hot coffee with milk, oats, buttered bread, and then cake.

The sea is marvelous. Dark green, translucent, seagulls fly around I stand and stare. Everything is like a dream. Marvelous freedom. There are no more electrified wire fences, no one is guarding us, we have as much to eat as we need.

I stand motionless on one side of the ship, I watch the gulls as they romp, the sea. As the waves roll by, I feel joy and freedom reach to the depths of my soul, yet my tears fall like rain. I would have been so thrilled if my dear mother were here with me. Papa is maybe already at home with my brother, but Mama? I will never see her again. I can no longer see a thing, I am no longer thrilled by that marvelous feeling of freedom. I am crying and all I can feel is an ache for my parents. My cousins comfort me until they, too, begin to cry.

At eight in the evening, we arrived at docks in the Swedish city of Malmö. When the ship came to a stop, they shot off a three-volley salute. Almost all the inhabitants of Malmö were there. A great hush fell. The royal minister then held a speech in Swedish and German and they sang the anthem, set off a rocket and with great gusto they cheered us, "Hurrah, hurrah." This lasted for nearly half an hour. We who were listening on board the ship had tears of joy coursing down our faces. Everyone is welcoming us; we who, eight days ago, were everywhere spat on, despised, beaten like the most vulgar beasts. This cannot be true, it's only a glorious dream, it's not possible. All of us wept, each of us had the same feelings. The Swedes noticed this. Some wept with us, they hugged us.

We did not understand what they are saying, but we felt they were consoling us. Later, consuls came from every nation and with us they sang their anthems. First a Dutchman because there were many of them. Later, from Czechoslovakia, Hungary, and then us, Yugoslavs. At that time the royal consul was still there from Yugoslavia, so we had to sing "*Bože pravde*" [the royal Yugoslav anthem]. We had no clue how things stood in politics.

It was after six in the evening when we disembarked from the ship. A bus was waiting for us. In front of the bus, they served us warm chocolate with cake and then we boarded the bus.

Malmö is a city that is beautifully lit; it is as light as if it were day. We drove for a long time. We finally stopped before a building. Here we got out, it was a bathhouse.

First we bathed in hot water, then they disinfected us with a white powder from head to foot. Then we went into another room and here a doctor greeted us, examined us, and sent those who were ill immediately to the hospital. They dressed the wound on my leg and we were given clean new clothes. We were ready after midnight and got back onto the bus.

We hadn't been riding for long when they informed us that we'd arrived. We got off the bus two at a time like well-behaved school-children. We looked around as if we'd never seen anything so nice in our lives. Twenty of us went into a room on the first floor. It was spotlessly clean. In the window, flowers. White beds. We stand there motionless, looking around. My heart is pounding in my throat. This is incredible for us. I look at the others, the same feelings are written on all their faces. Next to us stands the doctor and one of us asks him: "Sir, tell us how many of us to a bed?"

A silly question but he didn't laugh, he understood us because he knew how much we had suffered up until now. Softly and kindly in German, he told us:

"Dear children. You are in Sweden, in a country in which each person cares for you equally. There is no more wire to fence you in, you are free, you will eat and rest as much as you like. This is your room, 20 beds, and there are 20 of you. Come right in. Sleep well..."

Malmö, 3 May

At eight in the morning, a nurse arrived. "Good morning, how did you sleep? Are you hungry? I have brought you a ticket. Each person will get one, and with this ticket you will receive breakfast on the third floor."

We rose, assembled, and went in a line up to breakfast. A little room—there were six nurses inside and in front of each one was a pot and they were serving food. First, a spoon, knife, fork, then bread, two slices with butter. With one—a cup of cocoa and a milk roll, and the next one—a bowl filled almost to the brim with oats, semolina with compote, which are eaten together. The fifth nurse tipped a spoonful of cod-liver oil into our mouths, and the sixth, two doses of a small white vitamin and two iron pills. Our hands were loaded with food and we entered the dining hall that was beautifully furnished with flowers in front of each person. After breakfast I didn't feel full, and it wasn't just me but everyone. There were those among us who took advantage of the goodness of the Swedes, went through the line twice, didn't do what they were told.

At noon we saw the same nurses at lunch, where they gave us the following: bread, soup, roasted meat, spinach, compote, cake, more oats, and another spoonful of cod-liver oil. For afternoon tea we received cocoa with a milk roll. For dinner we were given the same thing we'd been given for breakfast.

4 May

After breakfast we went out into the yard. We mustn't venture farther than the yard, we are in quarantine for two weeks. Around the building there are Swedes. They toss us chocolate, clothing, and slips of paper with their addresses so we can write to them.

Each of us had something in her hands, chocolate as much as we could wish for. The four of us were always together. We stood in the garden and read the letters that they threw in to us.

A young schoolteacher who was with his two golden-haired children and wife threw in a letter and he asked us to write back and tell him where we were from, what we needed. We answered. He thanked us and left.

10 May

Each day has passed with more and more joy. The schoolteacher, Mr. Viking and his family are our daily visitors. True, they are on the other side of the fence, we are about fifteen feet apart. These people are as good as gold. Every day they bring us something else: cakes, candy, chocolate, dresses. This morning Mrs. Viking came alone and introduced us to another family, Mr. Lindal and his wife. They gave us flowers and a big box. In the box were silver spoons, a bottle of cream, hot black coffee, cups, hot milk, and milk cake—four pieces for each of us.

When we finished eating we returned it. How delighted they were when they heard from us that we'd enjoyed it. In the afternoon a woman we didn't know came and asked to see the Yugoslav women, speaking the Yugoslav language. We were very surprised, first because she had come and secondly because she knew we were there.

Eight of us responded. The lady introduced herself to us. A Serbian woman from Zagreb, her husband was the Swedish consul in Zagreb and when the war broke out they flew here by airplane. Here in Malmö they have a villa and they can hardly wait for us to be released from quarantine so she can bring us to her home.

We asked why she had dared to come? The nurse in another quarantine, where there were Dutch people, had contacted her voluntarily. She brought us southern food, the kind of food that we ate at home. Here everything is sweet. The bread is sugared, the fish, [illegible] and every kind of food that we make savory, they make sweet.

It was difficult for us to get used to it, but now we like it. Mrs. Teddy Vollin brought us cheese, kaimak, hot peppers, salt, and onions. We arranged it attractively on a plate and offered some to Mrs. Viking when she came. She was afraid and didn't dare swallow it down, and asked, "What is this—poison?" We laughed, it's a treat for us and for them, it's like poison.

11 May

They let us know early this morning that we should get ready to go into town. We were thrilled and jumped for joy. A bus was at the gateway to the yard. We are going for new clothes. We rode for quite a long time until we stopped outside of town by a huge store. We went in five at a time. They served us as if we were buying things with a lot of money.

First underwear, bras, socks, shoes, what kind, what color, what style, what heel, do you like this, that one is nice, try it on. If you don't like this one, try another. We chose what we liked and then a dress. Which one did I want? I didn't want silk because it isn't practical. I have only this one dress and when you get it dirty what do you do then? Wool will be too hot for me in the summer. Instead I'll take the cotton. The color is nice and it is practical and when it gets dirty, I'll wash it and it always looks nice. It might turn out that I don't have any dresses other than this one. After the quarantine we'll be going to work and it will come in handy. Almost all of us were thinking the same way. They are surprised we don't want the fancy dresses.

We also try coats, we choose whichever one we want, and with the coat, a matching hat.

Elegantly dressed, we got back on the bus. On we went. Near that store we got out again and went in to have our lungs x-rayed. Here a doctor examined us. We were done at about one o'clock and went back by bus. People stood along the way, cheering, "Hurrah!"

The bus stopped and we look out in surprise. We suddenly notice that flags are being raised in each town. It is over; the war is over, they are saying. The ceremony lasts for one-and-a-half hours.

And it's as if we're brave soldiers who came back from the front, victorious. They are cheering us as if that's what we are, throwing flowers down before us, covering the bus in flowers.

18 May

Fourteen days we've been in quarantine. With such impatience we waited for this day because they told us we'd be in quarantine for two weeks. Since they found among us someone who had typhus, they extended us for another fourteen days. Mrs. Teddy Vollin was here yesterday. She brought us many lovely things: a comb, a toothbrush, toothpaste, sewing thread in every color, buttons, a sewing needle, soap, perfume, and sweets. Everyone envied us. They loved no one as much as they loved us Yugoslav women. Today we received twenty envelopes from the Jewish community with ten crowns. We asked the nurse what one can buy with that.

It's a lot of money. For ten crowns you can get six pounds of chocolate or two pairs of fine stockings. Later Mrs. Viking came and brought us a Swedish language textbook with German translation. We are learning Swedish.

4 June

Another fourteen days went by and we were still in quarantine. The day before yesterday they gave us blood tests, there are still some among us who are ill.

Today we had a new guest who entered the quarantine, Mr. Nelson. He is Swedish and his wife is a Yugoslav woman who brought us two huge cakes, with twenty-four portions each. The eight of us ate them all, and he was so astonished that he was speechless.

In the evening I weighed myself, and after a month here I have gained seven pounds, now I'm up to 105 pounds. I am still very skinny, but I have a better complexion, I am beginning to look more like a person.

10 June

Today we heard what awaits us, or better said, we don't know precisely, all we know is that on the fourteenth we'll be released.

The four of us sat down on my bed and we talked. I was so disconsolate that I wept. Within four days we'd be released, in a state where we didn't know the language. We were without parents. What I need now are my Mama and Papa. What will become of us? Will we ever see our families? My brother? Papa? They, my cousins, couldn't console me because they, too, were weeping. I wasn't afraid of life; I know how to work, but I ached with longing for my parents, for home, for the warm circle of family. We knew no way to help destiny and must wait patiently.

12 June

The Dutch who are with us are all full of cheer. They are overjoyed, tomorrow they have a free day, and they are allowed to go into town to visit acquaintances wherever they like. Their consulate is rich and is taking them on the fourteenth to Gothenburg, a beautiful town. It will be like a summer vacation for them there. The [Yugoslav] royal consulate has collapsed and in its place, there is a new one representing Tito. The royal consulate asked us not to go to Tito's consulate, who won't treat us as nicely as they'd do, they'd take us to Gothenburg, too. But in vain they asked us to do this, we want to go back to Yugoslavia. We want to go back to our home!

We're a little sad, we will not be free. Tomorrow morning we'll be taken to Strängnäs. We'll not be able to visit our acquaintances, this pained us. In the afternoon Mr. Nelson came to visit. We told him all that weighed on our hearts. After that he went to see the director of the camp and asked to let us into town with him that very day. He was not able to permit it because it was only on the thirteenth that the quarantine ended and on the morning of the thirteenth, we were slated to travel.

He went to great lengths, running from one doctor to the next, until he managed to obtain permission to take us out by car from eight to ten that evening.

We were elated. Mr. Nelson phoned our acquaintances to let them know he'd be bringing us to them. At eight in the evening, we were met by two cars, in which we rode. First we go to Mrs. Tedi Vollin's. We stopped at their villa and she and Mr. Vollin were waiting for us out in front. They received us warmly. First they showed us the villa. A lovely garden full of roses, tropical flowers, tropical fruit, things that can't be found in all of Sweden, such as peppers, onions, currants. Then we went inside. The villa was on three floors. The upper floor was an apartment for their fourteen-year-old daughter, two rooms with a bathroom. The middle floor is the mistress's, also two rooms and a bathroom. And the ground floor is the gentleman's. Here he has a bedroom, hall, the dining room, and the front hall. In the hall they had set out a table for us. Everything with gold spoons and plates with a rim of pure gold. First coffee with whipped cream, five kinds of cakes, and along with this cocoa, chocolate, fruit, and not until we had eaten everything were we allowed to get up.

I looked at how much they were eating, the mistress drank her coffee and she ate a piece of pastry and nothing else. I wondered a little, why is she eating so little? I could have eaten everything that is here and she is already full.

As I was eating I was lost in thought and paid no attention to what they were talking about. In front of me I think of Mama cajoling me so earnestly into eating when I didn't want to with a story, a long one. I drank my coffee and I'm surprised she eats so little. She is used to fine food while I, we, we hadn't seen anything for seventeen months that was fine or good. We had starved. Is it any surprise that now we could not eat our fill? I was caught up in my thoughts about this until a great hush stopped me. The eyes of the others all turned to me. They saw that while I was eating, tears were coursing down my face, but I hadn't even noticed.

They didn't leave me be until I told them why I was crying. We were here for a long time, until after nine-thirty, but we had to be back by ten.

We said goodbye and got back into the car. Now we went to Mr. Viking's house. When the car pulled up they all came out, the whole family, the children, and even the grandmother, embraced and kissed us. They also wanted to show us their home. They had a very nice place, but it was small. Small rooms and a small yard. First there was a front hall, then the living room, dining room, elegant but very modest, then the bedroom where there was nothing but two wardrobes and two beds, and in the corners, a palm tree with only as much room as one needed to turn around. Then a little children's room which was full of toys, a little bathroom, and a little kitchen. In the dining room the table had been laid out for us. In vain we said we had already eaten, first at our accommodations, then with Mrs. Vollin, but we had to eat here too, the same coffee with whipped cream and cake. We were here for almost an hour and it was already ten-thirty and we still had to go to Mr. Lindall's. Mr. Nelson is driving us everywhere and what awaits us?

Mr. Viking came with us to Mr. Lindall's, riding his bicycle behind us.

Mr. Lindall lived near our accommodations. His was a nicer and larger flat than Mr. Viking's. They had a splendid piano. Mr. Viking plays the piano, and Alis and I sing. They offer us chocolate, we are afraid we'll have to eat here as well. After eleven we go on foot from Mr. Lindall's to our accommodations. Mr. Nelson, the Lindall family, and Mr. Viking accompany us. Out in front of the gate, the director and doctor are waiting for us. The director was nervous and he shouted at Mr. Nelson. "Do you not know Swedish law? That when you promise something this must be held to and you know that you will be severely punished for this."

Mr. Viking then told the director, "We will pay whatever the law requires. We will split it three ways. But please do not punish them, it's our fault they are late." They were very kind. We said goodbye and in we went.

13 June

At five a.m, we left the accommodations with a cousin. Outside, we were very surprised. Mrs. Viking and Mrs. Lindall were waiting for us, so early, with flowers. They came by bicycle. We got on the tram and they followed us on their bicycles to the station.

We all arrived there at the same time and they stayed with us until the train left. As we pulled away from the platform, they ran after us blowing kisses. Whoever we meet in the future, will we ever have friends as devoted as they are?

The train is lovely, as clean as a room. Next to each train compartment there is a small canteen. Eight of us, all Yugoslavs, sat in one compartment. A waiter came in and said something to the nurse who was with us. When the waiter left, the nurse said:

"Up there, there's a man who knows you've come from a concentration camp. He has bought you eight cups of coffee with whipped cream and sixteen slices of cake. He has asked you to go ahead and serve yourselves."

We ate and thanked him.

At five-thirty in the evening we arrived in Strängnäs.

Strängnäs-Rosega, 14 June

We were unpleasantly surprised. No one was waiting for us. We "high-hats" had already grown accustomed to warm welcomes. The nurse was also surprised. She said they'd called from Malmö to be sure they were expecting us. After we waited a quarter of an hour, they arrived. We got in. They drove about ten miles from Strängnäs to Rosega.

Rosega is a camp as efficient as that of the Germans. We almost burst into tears when we saw it. Mud, wooden pavilions. The kitchen looked like the crematorium in Auschwitz. What does this mean?

The Yugoslav consulate is poor and hasn't the money to take us to cities where we can spend our holidays. They built the facility only for the Yugoslav women.

Inside, it's not ugly. Clean. There are mattresses on the beds. Each of us was given two blankets, a mattress, a towel, soap, and a dress to work in.

Rosega, 15 June

We have grown used to this camp. The men's dormitories, where there are also Yugoslavs, are across from our building. They visit us often and inform us about the politics in Stockholm regarding the Yugoslav consulate. We get the latest newspapers and news from Yugoslavia.

Today I was complimented for the first time by a man. I felt myself blush, but luckily Gizela* arrived and called me in.

Gizela was assigned a task: she worked in the kitchen. The others helped. I didn't feel well. That's fine. I just stood inside. I sat alone on my bed, the days marched before me. Two months ago I would have given anything for something like this to happen, at least for an hour…We are never satisfied.

Now, food and rest no longer mean everything to me. I am nineteen years old. I haven't looked at myself in a mirror for over a year. What could I look like to have received a compliment?

---

* The names Gizi, Gizika, and Gizela all refer to the same person.

What was the man like? I can't remember. I know he was tall and that I didn't have the courage to look at him. What's going through my mind? Am I already thinking of men? Well...it's like I'm talking to myself. With my short hair, I must be ugly: he was only teasing (I got out of bed). I looked in the mirror. I have a man's haircut.

I brush it straight back (obviously I hadn't checked in a mirror). It is not right like this, it goes nicely like this, or differently, that's better. I style a little fringe around the ear, I look at the eyes, they are the same as they were, now a little yellowish because I'm ill. The face, a little too thin. I'm warm so my face is slightly flushed. My teeth are white. I scrub them with black coal. My leg aches, it's still bandaged on one place and it's swollen, which the doctor says is from eating too much too suddenly. Now I that know what I look like I'll put the mirror back. I had a look before me, what did I see? From the confusion and from the shame (shame, why?) I sat down because I was trembling. I thought of him then, what would someone say now to see me? He is here and sees me. "I have been watching you already for some time, you're beautiful, young lady, may I make your acquaintance?"

(Wait, why didn't you immediately say what you wanted, why were you staring at me like that? I don't wish to make your acquaintance, you have your friends; male company doesn't interest me at this time.) I found myself outside. I was red and hoped I wouldn't meet anybody along the way. I walked around the camp and went back into the room. He had already gone out and instead of him a girl came in who'd slept by my bed. "Why do you refuse to meet with this man? He's handsome, he already likes your company, he's a singer, he has a wonderful voice, he's from Paris…" "Why are you telling me this? He asked you to? Tell him I refuse to accept his company and that's that." She, too, went away.

Why did I do that? He certainly is handsome, what would be so wrong with stepping out with him? I'm no longer a child, why is this so strange? It's always nice, and we always want what we can't have. If the opportunity hadn't arisen for him to approach me perhaps I would have watched him, listened to his voice. I might have said to myself, how lovely that would be, I like the song, and all of that would happen, yet I won't. Why? I don't know.

20 June 45

I'm no longer ill, my leg has stopped hurting. I weighed myself and I'm up to 117 pounds, I've gained at least two pounds each week. What will happen if this continues? "What, I'm already afraid I'll be fat? Wasn't there enough starvation? That was then. How I will look when I'm fat?" (I often talk to myself like this.)

"Gizi, you know what I'd like today? I say that we exercise from now on every morning and evening, take walks in the afternoon. It's spring, beautiful weather. There are no mountains, but there are hills with nice slopes. It is pretty there. I was there once on a bicycle when I rode one that a little girl lent me. Will you, do you agree?" Hajnal—I know she won't. Alis's leg is hurting. But Gizela agreed immediately. Tonight the men have put together an evening of humor. We'll dress up—we've been in aprons all day—because after the performance there will be a dance. For the first time, a dance; does this help make it clearer? Because he will dance with me? If he were to dance and came for me would I go with him? I don't know, I think, yes.

He's sitting in the first row, talking with a lady. The lady beckons to me to join them. Where I drew the strength from I don't know. I knew [it was] because of him and still I went. I didn't want them saying I'm an idiot.

"Yes? You called me over, ma'am?" "Yes, I want to introduce you to Fritz." I turn to him and it's as if I'm seeing him for the first time. I give him my right hand. He asked me to sit. I sat. He didn't sit next to me, but right in front of me. I noticed he was looking at me, but I didn't want to show it. I talked with the lady. A little later she got up and the two of us were left there. He told me about his life, what suffering he'd been through in the life in the camp, and I told him the same things.

I didn't even notice, we talked from eight until ten and the dance had ended. They asked him to sing but he wouldn't, he wanted to be with me more, he said. That's why he didn't accept.

At ten-thirty all the men had to leave the women's accommodations and so we parted, but we agreed to continue talking tomorrow. When I got up I thought a little about him: he's nice, but I don't like him. There is none better looking than he is, why shouldn't I have fun with him a little?

30 June 45

Slowly I'm becoming more of a human being. Everything isn't passing by me as in a dream. I feel free and natural. When I'm in the company of men I don't feel I'm blushing, I speak easily and naturally with everyone. I often get together with Fritz. He is an intelligent and pleasant enough man, thirty years old. He likes me, I know, not because he said so, but I feel it. I enjoy his company, but I don't feel I love him. He often sings me songs, I like "*J'attendrai*" best, and that is why he sings it to me most often. He often tells me about his past life in Paris, where he worked for ten years as a bank clerk. He never used his voice at the camp in Germany and here he couldn't practice his trade. Today he visited, a little sad, yet glad to see me. "Lili, take a look." He handed me a letter inviting him to come to the coast near Gothenburg to a big café as a singer. He also plays beautifully on the violin and he has a friend who plays the saxophone and another, the accordion. All three are invited to appear tomorrow to perform for generous pay. I read the letter, gave it back, and asked him: "What have you decided?" "I'll take the job because I must; within two weeks I'd have had to leave as it is. Each of us can only stay for three months in the camp without employment. Now this provides me with the opportunity for a good job and I must take it. I'm glad, but at the same time I'm sad to be leaving you." He fell silent, looked at me and took my hand with both his own and asked softly: "Lili, could you be able to love me? I'd be happy if I felt you loved me a fourth as much as I love you. If you were to come with me as my wife, we'd be lacking in nothing and you'd have whatever you wanted, and with time you'd come to love me.

Think about it, Lili, for a little while, don't answer anything now. I am leaving right away, I am going to Stockholm and I'll be back tomorrow."

I was a little surprised that he'd gone ahead and declared himself so suddenly. I heard him out and gave him my hand in parting. He left immediately.

31 June 45

I told Gizika about him. I was curious what she would say. I was glad we shared the same opinion.

He's not for me. Perhaps I'd have a fine and beautiful time, with everything I could want, let's say the very best, but I wouldn't have matters most.

I long for a home, for a warm home with harmony, a marriage in which my future husband and I'd understand each other completely. "He" is all about appearances, a true aristocrat. The kind of woman who is for him is one who has the same sort of personality he has. That's not me.

He returned in the afternoon. He brought me a big box of chocolates, a red dress, stockings, and other odds and ends in a different box. I accepted this because I didn't want to insult him. Later we talked. I wanted to tell him what I'd decided but he asked me not to say. "I see on your face what you'll say. If you agreed, then you'd have said 'yes' right away. Now let me live at least in hope and please, when I write to you, answer with just two words, that you are healthy and alive. I want to know that much about you."

I promised him that. He left.

I didn't even write about June 23.

This is a major Swedish holiday, the biggest among the holidays and it is remarkable for the fact that the sun rises at one-thirty at night and sets in the evening at midnight, so there is only one hour of night. And even then it is not completely dark out, but like the way it is where we're from at about eight in the evening in summertime. So it's never all the way dark. The nights are always light as if it's never night at all.

The Swedes say that only in the south of Sweden, where we are, is there a moderate climate for eight months and a hot summer once every four years. Much like our country in May. Usually the winter is rainy, a little snow, and dark both day and night.

In the north, the climate is the reverse. Eight months dark and cold and four months light and moderate.

In the yard they arranged a huge cross of flowers and placed it right in the middle.

Around it are flags that are yellow, blue, with a yellow cross.

We went out. The Swedes showed us how they like to celebrate so we could do the same. Next to the cross there are musicians singing and playing Swedish folk songs. We joined hands in a circle and danced around in a circle and sang with them. After the dance was a party with cakes, coffee, and sweets.

3 July

Men often come to pick us up and go for walks with us. I go along but I'd be happier not to. I like being alone to dream, to build a future for myself. I think a lot about my father and brother. They're already surely waiting for me at home. Mama, sadly, I know where she is, but at least if I can find Papa and my brother. How wonderful that would be now to fly away and look for them, be together with them. There'd be nothing nicer than that and I don't feel like going for a walk...

Sometimes I think of Emil, where is he? At the camp I often sought him out. Whenever I saw men I'd look to see whether he might be there. But in vain. I loved him, who knows whether he's still alive? Or if he is alive, is he thinking of me? I am angry at him and he deserves it, but I'd forgive him if I were to see him. When I thought of him, that's what I decided.

5 July

Again, as always, it was announced abruptly that we should prepare to travel away from this camp.

For the trip we received, or better said, before we left we were given a dress, a set of underwear, a nightgown, and a pair of shoes with stockings. I already had quite a few nice dresses. We were each given a large suitcase by the Yugoslav consulate, eight bundles, and underwear.

At eight in the morning a bus took us from Rosega to Strängnäs. The train was ready to go at nine, so we didn't have to wait long to depart.

I'm on the train. I look out the window. Sweden is so beautiful. Modern, clean, peaceful, a marvel. The people are golden. Until now I thought only our families from Malmö were so good and kind, but every Swede is like that. At the first larger train station we come to they spotted us or someone told them where we were from, I don't know. People who were standing at the station cheered, threw flowers, chocolate, "Hurrah, hurrah." Is this quiet Sweden? Now it's not, now they're making noise the way we do at home. They don't have any [other] way to show their kindness to us. The train didn't stop for long, ten minutes, and when it pulled out of the station the people fell silent again, quiet like before.

At noon we pulled into a small town, but the train did not stop at the station. A little farther down the road, nurses from the Red Cross were waiting with hot food. They came into the train and handed everybody dishes and spoons. Then they brought something, I don't know what to call it, but we really liked it. Meat in brown gravy, sweet. Then they gave out cakes and tea served in paper cups.

The people from here gathered and they also behaved like the others.

At one on we went. We are traveling to the capital city of Sweden—Stockholm—and we will be going on beyond Stockholm right away, but I don't know where. I stand by the window and gaze out. I hear a Hungarian voice. When we come closer to the voice I'm surprised. Hungarian soldiers are standing outside and they're asking if there's anyone here from Hungary?

I didn't want to answer, but a Hungarian woman asked them what they're doing here. They answered, "We are in a camp here together with the Germans, as *Häftlingen* [prisoners], you can tell them at home we'll not be coming back." I don't know why they said that. Surely they like it here because here they aren't killing anyone.

We arrived at four. Stockholm is stunning. The sea reaches right into the middle of the city, a dock and bay in the center of town with a bridge. It is a marvel to behold. We got on a bus right away, we didn't linger, and the bus trundled us out of Stockholm. I look out again. The buildings are very tall, seldom does one see houses with less than five or six stories. I really like the recently built, modern part of town. The houses are in the shape of a villa that is ten or twelve stories tall. They are all built the same way. And they are painted the same way, strangely and wonderfully. From a distance they look as if they stand in a circle. We now went down into the lower town and here one could see better because the city climbs the slopes, it looks as if each row is painted the same way. Maybe they are. They seem so to me. We were soon fifteen miles from Stockholm.

Kummelnäs, 5 July

The most beautiful camp of all the ones we've been in until now. It's located on a dock by the water's edge, and at the camp the wooden blocks are surrounded by woods, flowers, and a garden. Yugoslavs who are staying at this camp came out to greet us. All men. There were older and younger men among them. Forty-three. Now that we've come we are seventy all told. We first entered an office where they registered us and then they escorted us to our block where we stowed our things and it was already six o'clock. We heard a bell chiming. "For dinner," as the people shouted who are from here.

We went out and followed the others. A wonderful room with big windows looking out over the sea and a flower garden. Inside there are tables and around each table, six chairs. We sat at two tables and women in white aprons offered us food, serving us. Dinner here is the same as the dinner in the other camps and I think in Sweden it is routinely so that in the morning there's breakfast, at noon they serve what we eat in our country for dinner, and in the evening they serve what we eat in our country at midday.

We were given soup, fried fish served with wine, milk, or yogurt. But the wine, it wasn't even wine, but a raspberry drink. At first you'd think that it is wine because it is bottled. Then cakes and semolina pudding with something like compote. Where we're from, compote is made from fruit but here there isn't much fruit or very little, so a kind of fruit that grows on a tree is peeled and cooked, and it's tasty.

After dinner we're free to stroll around as far as we feel like. That first evening we didn't go anywhere. They invited us but we said, "Tomorrow. Now we're tired."

7 July

It is nice here. I like everything and most of all, I feel the freedom. Here we truly are free, we are allowed to go wherever we like, just not to Stockholm without permission.

Kummelnäs is a place where rich people come on holiday from Stockholm. Here they have their villa and stay over the summer. This morning we sewed our own bathing suits, and in the afternoon we're going swimming.

I waited impatiently for the bell to chime, I wanted to be the first [to eat lunch] so I could be off swimming as soon as possible. I'd already announced to the others that next time we won't do it this way. One of us is to stay home each day, wait for lunch and bring it to the others so that way we can get down [to the beach] sooner.

The bathing area is quite far away. There is a beach closer by, but it's quite dangerous and not permitted. A ship often comes in to the dock.

The water is not exactly warm, it's colder. The sun is quite hot, much like it is in our country in late May, so it warms our swimming. On the other side of the bay, Swedish men and women swim completely nude. Morals among them are at a low level, but not everywhere. Where we swim no one is without a bathing suit, probably such swimmers are kept separate. There are also many mountains around the beach. So in our bathing suits we climb up and sunbathe. It was evening when we came back at eight. We weren't back in time for dinner, but we had something to eat anyway because we were hungry and we were given food by the others who still had some.

10 July

A lady and a younger woman came to our camp to meet the Jews. She, too, is Jewish and invited us to dinner at her home. We accepted.

At six in the evening they came to pick us up, the woman with her daughter. They lived quite far away. All the houses here are built of wood because the terrain in Sweden is so damp.

But they are built very nicely, especially inside. A full floor plan including a bathroom. We entered the hall. A long table was covered with dishes, all kinds of cakes, chocolate, and coffee, black and white with whipped cream.

The chairs are not around the table, but along the wall. The custom in their house is that the guests take a plate and serve themselves what they want and go back to their seat and they eat holding the plate that way. We did the same. First, I drank coffee with whipped cream, then I ate two slices of cake, but they didn't allow me to eat only two. There were other kinds of pastry, so I had some of these. It was about nine when they took us out into the garden. The garden was full of currants. We ate the currants. At about ten they escorted us back.

15 July

We have been in Kummelnäs for ten days. I'm feeling well, I experience each moment that passes with delight. If I were with my parents and brother, I'd say that nothing could hurt me anymore and that I'd already forgotten the evil. How strange fate is, that evil can be so quickly forgotten, but the beautiful and the good cannot. How beautiful it would be to feel my heart brim with joy, to enjoy this wonderful freedom, this opportunity, but what I have in my heart will pass. I will never again be able to feel my heart full of joy. Yesterday evening was nice. We went down to the dock and three of us got into a boat: Juro, me, and a man who rowed. It was nine and not dark yet, it was half-dark and toward Rosega the sky was lighter. The swells were not big, the most pleasant possible, and the sea is bedecked with the ships embarking for Stockholm every five minutes, so when one passes, the next one already appears. The ships are three stories high with many windows lit. The ships travel quite far from the camp where the seas are deep, because near the camp there are shallows.

I can't see the camp at this point, we're so far off. We don't dare go near the ships, but we aren't too far from them. The air is mild; I feel a gentle breeze as if it's caressing me. I have no complaints. Nothing could be nicer. I like it, except what's in my heart...

Why can't I tell my beloved family about this bliss, my joy? How glad they'd be, they'd surely want that. "Come to us, darling girl, you've suffered so much. May God-given joy, contentment, and happiness follow you always."

That's what they'd say and they'd kiss me, and I'd thank them with tears of joy and kiss their hands.

But that's only a dream, a marvelous dream, a marvelous fantasy that will never be.

When Juro talks to me and tells me stories, I don't hear anything. Before me are these thoughts and, wrapped in them, I feel better. I'm glad and I enjoy myself, but never completely.

At around eleven we got back. He doesn't understand me. His parents are waiting for him, I know, though he's not so sure. I didn't divulge anything when he asked me how I was feeling. "Fantastic!" I wasn't lying, I was telling the truth and I showed a glad face. He doesn't see into my heart (though he's close).

He's close; what does that mean? I ask myself now at a moment when I've already written this. I feel I like him. Until now I hadn't thought about it so I didn't mention it. But now that this is the case I'll write about him.

On July 12, he came to our camp from Lund. He didn't come alone, with him were another four men. I was standing at the window and I watched him. The others who also noticed him said in a low voice, "That one in the navy-blue jacket is cute."

I was angry at him because he walked right by us, by me, and didn't even look inside. Down there the others gladly stood and talked. That's strange, what I immediately noticed in myself. Why was I angry? What for? He doesn't even know me, he couldn't… All day long I didn't see him. The other men immediately came to our block and were chatting. I didn't even listen to them. If he were here? Maybe I would've. As far as I can tell, Vali also likes him, but she's not as free as I am with asking: "What is that fifth man who was with you up to?" "Him? He doesn't like the company of women, he sits on his bed and reads." I did the same.

The next day at noon we went to lunch. The four of us sat at a table and since we were last in we had to sit where there were seats. Two men were sitting there and we joined them. He was one of them and the other was a man we'd already met. He was nice, friendly, and jocular. He understood all sorts of things and wanted to handle everything, so they nicknamed him "Consul." He introduced us to the other man. During the lunch we talked a little. Hajnal sat next to him and I sat next to Consul. Backwards. Hajnal really likes Consul, which was obvious right away.

I didn't so much as look at him. Hajnal talked with him while I talked with Consul. Consul suggested we go for a little walk after lunch, and that I should invite Hajnal. Juro would also come. I didn't want to; I don't know why. I wasn't in the mood.

After lunch Hajnal agreed. They asked me, but I didn't want to go. At that they all pounced on me. First he said, "Why won't you? Fresh air is nice, now after the rain, it will refresh you." "Not now, no," says Gizika. She wouldn't give up, "Come on, we're all going, you can't stay by yourself!" I went after all. The four of us walked in single file, Hajnal, Consul, me, and Juro. We didn't walk long as a foursome. Consul and Hajnal went off by themselves, so we two were left alone together. We walked by the flowerbeds, he leaned over and picked me a few blossoms and gave them to me. He told me about his life. He'd come from Lund where he'd been bedridden for six weeks with typhus. He was as skinny as a skeleton. Later when he recovered, he convalesced. He told me more: that he spent three weeks with women and from that day forth he cannot abide the company of women, they behave so badly and immorally.

"Why did you ask me along if you dislike the company of women?" I ask. "I don't know," he answers. "Somehow with you I don't feel that way." "With the others?" "I don't know. Lilika, let me spend time with you. Talk about yourself a little." "No, now I won't. I'm going back, I'm not in the mood. I was in a bad mood and you could've noticed that right away." He asked me to stay, but I didn't want to.

He escorted me back and said: "I'm going back too, and I'll read, goodbye. I'd like for us to talk a little, please let me stop by and pick you up tomorrow." "I'll see," I answered, and "Goodbye." I don't need him, the conceited ape. He doesn't like the company of women, what does he expect from me? That's what I was thinking when he left. I lay down and picked up a book and read.

13 July

He was already at our place in the morning around ten. I was sewing, I am adapting a dress. He sat near me and watched. I don't know why, somehow, I felt antipathy toward him, even though he is, in fact, nice.

I despise conceited men and I remembered that when he announced that he didn't like the company of women, I had the answer ready: "What are you doing with me, then?" He sat for a long time in silence, because I didn't say anything when he asked me: "Lilika, are you angry at me? Or does something hurt? Why are you in such a foul mood?"

"It's not that I'm in a foul mood, Juro, I've nothing to talk about. I apologize that I'm sewing, I want to finish it."

"If I knew how, I'd help you finish it as soon as possible but since I don't know, I won't bother you. Would you allow me, Lilika, to come by this afternoon? Around five? May I?"

I agreed. Why? Only because I don't want to be the topic on everyone's lips. They all go out for a walk, but I stay behind? We'd immediately combine something because he'd probably have stayed in his block, so I chose to agree.

I finished the dress I was sewing and went out that afternoon wearing it. A blue skirt with embroidered red designs, a red blouse, and a belt. Everybody liked it. He too, he said.

The air was mild, not too hot. The most pleasant, really. The two of us went for a walk with them. I was in good spirits, which he really liked. We hadn't gone far from the camp when I ran into Consul riding a bicycle. He stopped and asked me, "Where is Hajnal, at the block?" "Yes," I answered and stared fixedly at the bike. Just as I did a month ago when I first saw food, and now I recalled that. Would I still know how to ride a bike? I felt a powerful urge to ride really far, as if flying. If only I knew how, I'd ride all the way back to my family, day and night without stopping, but that was pure fantasy. At least I could try a little to see if I still knew how. I felt like a child whose every wish is granted when he handed the bike to me. When I went to sit on it I completely forgot I hadn't been alone, but once seated on the bike I said goodbye to him. I rode it uphill and didn't even feel the strain of the slope and that I'd gone a long way until a moment when I got off and caught my breath. The air was mild, not too hot, like always. I looked down, surveyed the countryside, the sea, how still it was, the sun shining on the water. From here it seems so marvelous, it seems that it would be wonderful to stay here forever. No, it was only in that moment, the breathtaking surroundings, the nature, that the romance suited me, when I was alone. I sat back on the bicycle and rode back. Halfway down I met my friends. Hajnal, Consul, Zlati, Ljulika, Bogdan, and Juro. Zlati ran after me and shouted, "Stop! Let me have a turn." I couldn't get down off the bike. "When I get to the flat part." But she wouldn't let me pass, "No, let me have it now!" She was still a ways off and stood in front of me, and though I wanted to dismount, I couldn't stop the bike. I tumbled to the ground, my head was in a ditch. If they hadn't pulled me up I wouldn't have been able to scramble to my feet. My whole leg was bloody. Juro's face at that moment, the way he looked, I will never forget it. I didn't feel any pain, but my leg really was something to see, so much blood that it was horrible. He put me back on the bicycle, sat on it himself, and took me straight to the doctor. We didn't find the doctor in at his office. I sat on a bench and Juro raced around, frantic, and went into the clinic, nobody there either. Afterward he inquired about the doctor's private address, went to his home, and later he told me the doctor had been entertaining company when Juro came in and pleaded with him to come at once. The doctor thought, he said, that someone was at death's door. He bandaged up my leg. First he washed it, that hurt a lot, Juro stood behind me and held my head tenderly as if he were caressing me with his eyes. He followed my every sigh as if he were my mother. I was in terrible pain, but I had to admit to myself that even if I had felt antipathy for him before, now I really loved him. When the doctor finished bandaging my leg (like a white sock wrapped from top to bottom), he asked, indeed begged, me to tell him sincerely what Juro was to me. Brother or husband? "You don't see such a tender moment like this except in the movies, how he behaved. No need to answer, I just want to give you my honest advice: you should respect and love this young man because he loves you sincerely. As a practitioner I saw this with my own eyes."

Juro asked me what the doctor had said, and I told him the truth.

18 June 46

For five days my leg was in bandages and for those days I was never bored. I had constant company and Juro was always by my side. He told me about his whole past and the future he hopes for, about school. I feel I love him. He still doesn't say so to me but I feel it.

Today I walked around a little and limped a little with him, but in a few more days it will be all better.

20 June

As if my leg had never been injured, it had healed completely. This evening we went out onto the water in a boat. He rowed and sang. I was light-hearted and happy. It was nine o'clock, moonlight, the boats going to Stockholm were like a caravan. Every five minutes you could see another one, three-stories tall, all lit up, and the sea was still. We let the boat float around. Juro didn't row, he sat next to me. For a time he was quiet and looked at me. I wasn't looking at him. I felt it and heard it when he said: "Lilika, something…" Then he stopped when he saw I wasn't reacting. I knew if I didn't come up with a topic quickly maybe both of us would confess we loved each other, but I didn't want it to come to that yet, so I talked about something with him, I can't remember what, all I know is we kept talking, and he told me about Sušak, and the Adriatic, and at midnight we parted.

25 June

Today is Monday. We were given permission to go into Stockholm, but only four of us. We agreed that Gizika, Zlati, Juro, and

I would go, and I was already prepared when Ilika came and asked if one of us would give her a pass because she had been waiting so eagerly to go. I gave her mine, and since Juro wasn't there just then he had no idea. They left (I was sure he'd be angry which would be no surprise, I don't know why I gave her the pass). All day I am alone.

I write. What is there to write about? Him. I keep writing about him. I often feel I love him, and often, like now, for instance, I feel it's better that way. A person shouldn't spend too much time in someone's company, especially when the attraction on one side is greater as was true in our case. It is difficult for me to love someone, but if I do begin to love, I love sincerely. Perhaps if I were to see him less often, I'd miss him and he'd be more attractive to me. I love him now, but I wasn't thinking yet of love. The time for that would come, I was certain. One day? When? It will come in its own time and from that moment on I'll know and I'll be clear about what I feel for him. Now to write a little about the camp.

Our block is clean, each of us has our own bed and keeps it tidy. We're given a clean sheet every week. Breakfast is from seven to nine in the morning, lunch is from noon to two, and dinner from five to seven. The hall where we dine is beautiful. The windows look out over the open sea, there are tables and around each are four chairs and in every corner and on the windowsills, palms and flowers. Every day one of us women is assigned to help in the kitchen, so once a week I have my turn. The same goes for the men. The women serve the "guests," and after lunch the men wash the dishes and the women dry them. The food is not the best, at least to me, because almost every day we have fish. And the food is usually all sweet, while our cuisine is savory.

It is now four and they will probably be back by evening.

I stopped with my writing. They came home at six, Juro is probably angry at me. He didn't come in and they told me how moody he was. What will I tell him? Why did I do that? I don't know. I don't even want to think about it. I'll wait and see.

28 June

Yesterday he asked me to go with him for a walk after lunch. I agreed. I expected him to ask me right away why I did that on the twenty-fifth, but he didn't. He talked to me about all sorts of other things as if nothing had happened. After dinner we went on with our walk. We walked to the woods, listened to the crickets chirping, looked at the stars, the countryside. Mostly we were quiet and didn't talk. We came to a bench and sat. He took my hand, bowed his head and, as if talking to himself, quietly and calmly he asked me, "Lilika, tell me sincerely, do you feel how much I love you?" He looked at me, and read from my eyes what I wanted to say, and before I said anything he said, "Thank you, I forgive you everything because I must. You'll tell me yourself why you did that when you feel you can." I felt something choking me, I felt so much if only I knew how to say it, and there was just one word on my tongue and in my feelings, "I love you, Juro." But I didn't say it. I stood up and on we walked. He started again. "I have been feeling that I love you for a while. At least allow us to dispense with formalities and switch to using the intimate form of address. Could you? I could and it would be easier for me, to love you as I've never loved anyone. But I've waited until now, ever since that happened when you tricked me, or I don't know what to call it because I don't know the reason. I felt how badly I missed you and how much I love you, Lili. Tell me sincerely what you feel, don't leave me in pain." I don't know what I said. He kissed me and I ran away from him and back to the building. They asked me why I was so upset and I begged them not to ask.

29 June

I hate him. I can't abide his company. I cannot even think about last night. I couldn't eat breakfast today. I lost my appetite when I thought of what happened last night. I'll tell him today I don't want his company. Why? I still feel I love him, so why do I hate him? I don't know, I'll continue [writing] tonight.

We were together, just the two of us, we walked, talked, and then what I wanted to say, what I had been thinking about all day, I didn't tell him. Why? I have a reason.

Today after lunch they announced we'd be going tomorrow to work in Eskilstuna, and whatever we earn will be ours. As of tomorrow we're free. If we ask for or need help they will help us, the consulate of each of our nations will be at our service.

They announced the same thing to the men that day, but the men weren't going to Eskilstuna, but to Stockholm.

That is my reason. It came abruptly, and ever since, or because of that, no matter how much attraction and hatred I felt for him all that day, I couldn't remember those feelings once I was with him in the evening. Both of us were in a sour mood. It often seems to me that I am thrilled and so grateful for the opportunity, and yet at the same time when we think perhaps we won't be seeing each other again, I'm sorry we'll have to part. I was already thinking about this before I even started to write. What would I say and which option would I choose? If I were able to, would I stay with him at the camp or go off with the others to work? (Because if I were to want the same thing he wants, we'd get it, under the condition that we couldn't return to Yugoslavia when the time comes for that, but we'd stay here in Sweden). If I were to stay, my feelings that I'd begun to feel for him for the first time since yesterday would surely change. Not maybe, but definitely. I'd love him sincerely, and that, for me, is love. Marriage would follow from this sincere love, maybe even before we made it home, because I'd only be able to return to Yugoslavia after a few years or once I'd earned something so we would have had enough money.

I didn't need to look too long for my answer because I'm writing what I feel. I won't choose that path. How peculiar I am. And how grateful I am to fate that it created me to be this independent. That I know how to think independently and realistically, that no one can sway me, that I know myself, that I am in command of my feelings, to adapt to whomever I'm with…what am I writing? I'm lying! This is not true! What? I know myself and how to be in command of my feelings? I know how to adapt to those I'm with?

[Only] when I am in company where I feel well, and that's my mistake. That's why I am mostly quiet when I'm in company.

But that isn't what I started writing about. The reason: first, I'm Jewish; he's a Serb. Now Gizika says: "By the time we return home and back into the old swing of life there won't be any…we'll no longer feel the difference between faiths," but I don't believe this and not only do I not believe it, I feel this is the only, the first and last reason! Because the more I think of him, the more I love him. That's why I'm peculiar. Because I know I'll be stronger than this feeling that usually drives a person and is called "losing one's mind."

I continue: both of us are in foul moods. Especially him. "I feel, Lili, that you feel my thoughts, which are so heavy that they're choking me. I can't express, Lili…'Lili' is just a name and it's strange, so short and yet so hard for me to say, don't laugh and don't make me laugh. I remember my grandmother. As I already told you before, my grandmother really loved me. When I was seventeen she told me for the first time…" "I know, Juro, let that be, please!" "Lili, please let me talk, I need to talk because it helps me. Our parting will come in any case and these will be painful moments for me, but if we don't change the subject then those moments will come sooner. Leave it, Lili, let me be happy. Let's walk together until we go our separate ways, so I can watch you smile the way you were smiling when I was talking about my grandmother. Then you were so dear, you laughed as I did about her, please, Lili, let me keep talking, that will be better." (We were walking across the grass to a tree.)

"Fine, Juro, you're right, talk, talk to me." He hugged me, I rested my head on his shoulder, I listened and laughed. And in my heart? I loved him as I never had before. We sat that way for a long time and he kept talking, moving from one topic straight to another, from his grandmother to his parents, from school to love. He talked about his friends, his teachers, his high school graduation, until he came back to where he'd started. Then we looked at one another and laughed. Suddenly, nearly at a run, we hurried back into the camp because it was after eleven when every gate was shut.

What do I feel now? Do I still hate him? No, I love him and I kissed him, and he, "How I love her." Tomorrow morning we're leaving and he promised that he'd come to the bus, even if I asked him not to. They're leaving on the boat before noon.

Eskilstuna, 30 July

The time came for farewells and we parted. I promised I'd write him this very day and I did, but only briefly, on a single sheet of paper. I needed to be the one to write first because he didn't know my address and I wrote to him at the address of the Yugoslav consulate because that's where they were staying.

I won't write further today—that's why I wrote just a brief note to Juro, it is already late and I'm tired.

4 August

We have a beautiful apartment. It is on the third floor: three rooms, a kitchen, and a bathroom. The rooms have parquet floors.

There is some furniture. The kitchen, it's small, with a gas stove, a built-in wall cupboard and seating along the wall.

There are eight of us. In the evening the apartment looks like the camp did, a lot of rooms packed with beds. But during the day there are two sofas, we fold the beds up and store them in the wall. Like in the movies. Beautiful, tidy, and practical.

We work at a glove factory. Alis is the housekeeper, she cooks for us. At noon we come home for lunch and at one, we return. It is a little far. We always need to hurry and Alis always has to be prompt so she can be waiting for us with lunch ready. We begin at seven in the morning. Everyone comes to work by bicycle. The ones who are older, who find it strenuous to cycle, go to work on motorized bikes. So at seven there is heavy traffic, but from eight until noon everything is dead quiet, and at one [the traffic picks up] again, while we work from one to five. Every person works and every person is educated. Everyone has at least some schooling, because in their country everyone is under orders to complete a secondary-school education. Afterward, no matter what training they pursue, they are equals. Farmers go by car to work and return home to their modern-designed villa.

The work is a little difficult for us, but only until we get used to it. I have to keep the machine running. It runs on electricity, but that is why I am always hunched over, hurrying to finish as much as possible because we work on quotas.

We have and earn a decent salary, which we share in equal parts with Alis.

10 August

Juro writes me every other day. I answer him regularly. For instance, today I wrote that he must not be thinking so much about me because he'll destroy Sweden. This is because he wrote that he'd broken twenty-five crystal dishes. They wanted to fire him, but they forgave him. I study his letter and I don't understand: "...the days are going by and one after another they pass, always boring, but as of today I'm working with joy because..." Three dots and no ending. As of today? What is today? At the end of the letter he asks me to forgive him for being so childish but on "...the fourteenth you'll find out, perhaps even sooner. I want to surprise you, so our shared joy will be all the greater because I know you think I might turn up to surprise you, but you know, Lili, that is, sadly, impossible, as it is for you. You'll find out soon, my darling," that is how he closes.

In vain I wonder. I don't know, it seems silly to me or really as if he is writing childishly, but he is neither silly nor childish, maybe—now I'm laughing—"He's lost his mind."

14 August

On the twelfth I found out. Tomorrow all eight of us are going to Stockholm. On the eighteenth our transport leaves for Yugoslavia. That is what Juro already knew on the tenth!

We're getting ready. We didn't go to work today, the director is furious with us, but it's not our fault. He has every right to be, he had a lot of expense with us, he furnished the apartment, paid us for three months, bought the machines and now we're leaving so abruptly. He begged us to stay in Sweden, he brought us newspapers, told us about what Yugoslavia is like, but this was wasted on us. We want to go home, my father and brother are waiting for me at home. I am going and each of us feels the same. With our money, we bought clothes. All the nicest things because we have plenty of money.

15 August, Stockholm

Juro was waiting for me at the station. We were both elated. He was in an especially gleeful mood. "I am by your side again, Lili, that is my first reason to be happy, and the second, I don't have to wash the dishes, fabulous. Imagine Lili, what I did yesterday. An elegant man sat down in a brand-new gray suit in the café where I'd been washing dishes for two weeks and ordered the finest and fanciest entrees, but his one request was that he be served on double dishes. Who was the gentleman? Me!"

We laughed all morning. He had so much of the charming past of Stockholm to tell me about. "And you found this boring?" I asked him, astonished. "Yes, it all seemed boring, but now that you're by my side everything's different."

This was my second time in Stockhom on the same street, but it didn't seem the same, as if I'd never seen it before. I'm so pleased,

I'd like to see everything at once. Juro already knew the city well, so we went for a little walk and visited the famous sites.

It was almost evening by the time we reached the consulate. They had already been looking for us, but they forgave us.

16 August

At ten in the morning we left the consulate. There were almost 200 of us, lined up in groups of ten. We went along the main street to the station with song and music. The Swedes cheered, flung flowers, "Hurrah!" "Cheers!"

At noon our train pulled out. We had plenty of room so we could lie down because it was only the next day that we'd be reaching Gothenburg and the ship that was waiting there for us.

There was music in our compartment, so we all spent the afternoon together. At about seven everyone else dispersed and we set ourselves up for sleeping. We wanted to stretch out, but there wasn't enough room for that. First, the women lay down, leaving room for the men either on the floor, or in the net designed for light packages. (So considerate.) Juro curled up in the net across from me. We talked for a while and I fell asleep.

At about nine I opened my eyes; Juro was standing next to me. Surprised, I asked him why he wasn't sleeping. "I can't!"

It was warm. I got up, we went out and both of us stood by the window and looked at the way the train was rushing through the night.

We stood there, arms around each other, and talked a long time until we went back in and I went back to sleep.

Gothenburg, 17 August 45

We traveled for exactly one day. We went straight to lunch from the station. In the afternoon we stuck together and went to the docks.

This evening at ten the ship set sail for Germany.

18 August

We slept on a lower deck, each in our own group. Early in the morning, Juro came to fetch me for us to go up together. It was cold up on the top deck. Juro went back to get my coat. I slipped it on and we stood at the railing and enjoyed marvelous nature. The sea was an entirely dark green as the ship went along. As it sliced through the water it looked like silver, pure and transparent.

We're heading home. I am choked with tears, pain in my soul, and as far as I can tell, Juro is feeling the same thing. Seagulls are flying around us, the weather is growing warmer, I didn't even notice how long we were standing there in silence, but we are no longer alone. It [the deck] was almost full, we went back and joined the crowd, had our picture taken, sang and danced.

We landed. English army with trucks was waiting for us there. They trucked us fifteen miles to our camp.

There are about 2,000 of us Yugoslavs here. The camp consists of tourist tents. In the tent there is straw and two blankets per person. The tent is spacious so there are twelve of us in it. Each of us was given a ten-pound package with soap, cigarettes, chocolate, cookies, canned food, cheese, and so forth.

25 August

We have been here a week. They say we will be continuing on our way on September 1 for Yugoslavia. We have plenty of good food and the countryside is nice. There are woods and a lake. I often go with Juro for walks, which is my only pleasure.

Tomorrow evening there will be a concert, violin, and after that we women who have nice voices will sing. Among us there are people who don't want to go back to Yugoslavia. They [the Communists] are our enemies, so they say. They often quarrel and now they are working to keep us from holding the concert, but we are not giving in, so we're rehearsing and preparing.

1 August

In the same trucks we return to the city. A train is already waiting for us. Only freight cars and in the cars, straw, and an electric motor is running it. Along the way we were also given five-pound packages from England, so that we have enough to eat.

Juro is always with us, with me. I love him and I miss him when we aren't together. He feels the same way.

Jesenice, 3 August

We arrived in Yugoslavia. We were pleasantly disabused of our expectations. As we traveled through Germany, we saw what Germany looks like, how devastated it is, and from what we'd heard from the Swedes who described Yugoslavia, we thought Yugoslavia would look like that as well, but we were pleasantly disabused.

We spent a whole day in Jesenice. We went to the Sava River with Juro, thinking we'd go for a swim, but I didn't want to, so he didn't either.

Ljubljana, 4 August

We arrived in Ljubljana. Time for our farewells, it is seven in the evening. There are only two hours left for us to be together; his train for Sušak [is leaving], that's where he is going.

We stepped down from the train, just the two of us, while the others stayed behind. We sat in the grass. It was so painful for us to part that we were at a loss, he and I, for how to find the words. I cried. He understands me, he's faced with the same thing I'm faced with.

I'd been accustomed to the love of my parents and fate had, sadly, separated me from them, but in hopes that we'd see each other again, I went through misery and that was what kept me alive. Fifteen months had passed, all that time. Now in Sweden, I'd come to love Juro. I first felt a brotherly love for him, later tenderness, sincerity, a sort of mother's love, and then later love, and now, again we were parting, and who knew, perhaps we'd never see each other again. Who was waiting for me at home? I was heading, blindly, home, but I didn't know what I'd find and whether I'd find anyone and whether I'd feel at home. I'm crying and in my thoughts are these feelings. Juro is thinking the same things except he's thinking out loud. He's talking to me, he has more hope that he'll find his family because they stayed home when he was taken away, he loves me sincerely, and the only thing he feels sorry about is me.

The time passed quickly. Already his train was about to leave, when Juro lifted me up as if I were a weightless package and put me through the door into the freight car.

As long as I could see him I followed him with my eyes and finally he disappeared. This was very hard for me, harder than any parting, but there was nothing I could do about it.

Zagreb, 5 August

We disembarked from the train and they shut us up in the quarantine section of the Zagreb station. People came around the quarantine. We ran over to them just as we were used to doing; visitors always brought us something. We hoped they'd give us something Yugoslav, but we were unpleasantly surprised when all of them asked us the same question, "Have you any chocolate?"

Later people came from the Jewish community and brought us a list, a roster of all the Jews from Yugoslavia. Each of us looks for our family members, we hear cries of joy from those who find at least someone of theirs, and sobs from those who find no one. Sadly, this is the case for the four of us.

I sat alone, grieving, far from the others. At noon they called me to lunch, but I didn't go. Without hope, without a will to live, I stayed alone, sitting in the same spot.

Where was I to go? I'd follow my three cousins, they consoled me, we would work and always be together like four sisters. That is all well and good and I'm grateful to them for that, but the ache in my heart wasn't eased, settled, by these words. In the evening we left Zagreb.

Sremska Mitrovica, 6 August

We got down again off the train and went into town. They took us to the barracks, to a room with straw and said we'd stay there for a week, until they regulated us.

12 August

It is boring here and we're impatient. We go swimming and for walks because swallowing all this dust is impossible. The food is bad, only corn, bread made of corn flour. For dinner we cook meals of corn. All this would be bearable somehow if only our spiritual pain were the least bit eased. Every day the same sighs from everyone's lips: "How much longer like this?"

14 August

At last the time has come and we leave Mitrovica.

16 August

We journeyed to Novi Sad for two days. The four of us together went to the Jewish community office. Here we found people we knew who received us with sincere, painful news.

First, my cousins heard their oldest brother had died, that there was no one waiting for them. That was enough. Gizika fainted. They weep, we weep.

Sadly, I received similar news. No one knows anything about Father, while my brother was last seen in Bergen-Belsen. He didn't want to wait after liberation for a transport to bring him home, so he set out on his own through the woods, hungry, and perhaps he is no longer alive.

Touching and sad that they greeted us this way. We'd have heard the sorrowful news sooner or later; they shouldn't have told us right away, but regardless, perhaps it's all for the best. It makes no difference anyway.

I went into town with my cousins and on the way ran into Ela who greeted me with a kiss and a smile as if she were glad to see me, but she didn't invite me to stay with her. A little later we met up with our uncle who was thrilled, he grabbed us and carried us off to his house. He offered us all he had. He had aged terribly, poor Uncle Mikša Bači, Leona had gone away, Jančika was with him. About my brother he said the same thing they told me at the Jewish community office. I didn't stay long.

I left and went to Gizika's. She was very glad, sincerely so, which I could see right away. She asked me to invite my cousins to come to her place and stay with her as long as we liked.

We had dinner at Mikša Bačka's and afterward we went off to Gizika's.

17 August

Today in the afternoon we called Faninenika in Senta. After dinner I took to bed because I wasn't well.

18 August

I'm happy again, my wish has been at least partly fulfilled. Yesterday evening, after I called, when my brother heard I was in Novi Sad, he hopped onto a truck and came to find me and at midnight, he reached Gizika's where I was. First Gizika woke, as did Pišti. They were pleased as could be because they'd had no news of my brother. When my brother came in, Pišti came to my bed to wake me. They knew I'd jump for joy if I learned right away, although I might hurt myself, so they were cautious. "Darling, wake up, time to get up, it's midnight and the train's about to leave." I opened my eyes and was surprised that the time had passed so quickly, I was about to get up when I caught sight of my brother who was poised to kiss me. I started crying and shouting "It isn't true, this is a wonderful dream, isn't it? Tell me!" I hugged him, kissed him, and the two of us wept.

I am so grateful to fate for not leaving me alone. My uncle Batja from Bačka Palanka is also alive, and he is impatiently waiting for us, my brother told me, in Senta.

My brother is an American soldier. And now something sorrowful, there's never joy without pain: he wanted to show me the documents he'd received from his former major that he could take me back with him, when he noticed his documents were not in his pocket. He was glum, but then we all lay down to sleep, and early in the morning, at four, he went out with a bicycle to search for his documents.

Unfortunately, he searched in vain. He came back at ten and at two we all sat together on the train for Senta. We arrived in the evening. All of Senta was at the station: the Jews, the [illegible] family, Endre, Joška, and Uncle were waiting with a cart. The others sat in the cart, and my brother, uncle, and I walked. The whole way I talked, hugged my brother and uncle.

At Faninenika's we had dinner and lay down to sleep.

Senta, Saturday, 21 August

I received a telegram from Juro: "Why haven't you been writing?" I'd promised him I'd write first because I knew his address, but hadn't yet gotten to the point when I could write. My brother was surprised and asked who this man was, and he was alarmed. After one hour, an express letter. I was so glad, and read through it several times with joy. During that time my brother was very sad. In vain I talked to him and lied, saying Juro was just a good friend from Sweden, but he's smart, glum, and his mood didn't brighten. He didn't even want to taste the food. At lunchtime it was the same, while in the afternoon he burst into tears and got up to leave. I went after him and at the gateway both of us wept.

He told me: "I know everything and understand it all. This man, if he weren't serious he wouldn't have written and sent a telegram, and even if I don't know what's in the letter, I know that this man, as soon as you answer him, will be here. If not right away, then in no time he'll come to Senta to see you. You'll walk with him through town and when the Jews see you what will they say? Whose daughter are you? Who are you? What have you become? If you persist with this and don't respect our late parents then with pain I will have to leave you because I couldn't remain at your side, with you, on whom until now I've placed all my hopes, but apparently I respect our parents more [than you do]."

We wept, I pleaded with him not to talk that way, that he couldn't understand me, I promised him everything, that I'd never write back to Juro, and finally he calmed down a little.

This is so painful for me. I must forget Juro. No, that's impossible. I still love him and he deserves better, he will suffer if I don't write. I will lie to everyone, let everyone else be happy, but me? I'm marked to suffer; I'm already so used to suffering.

1 September

I receive a letter from him every other day. My brother thinks I'm not responding. I lie, as I decided to do.

I write to Juro. The first letter, with the words he expected; the second, a little cooler, I'm disconsolate. The third, today, which I also am writing in secret, alone, sends false impressions of Senta and at the end, "Next time I'll answer your letter. I have gotten so carried away with relating my impressions that I've no more space left."

I feel awful for him, he's already suffering, but isn't it enough that I'm miserable? Slowly, through several letters, he'll figure it out as I write to him, and I'll let him think that distance has driven us apart. It's easier for me if I think that at least he's hopeful and he's not miserable because of me. I often feel I should be honest, but I can't. I love him still, and I'd like it more if through our letters I could change our love to friendship, and that we could stay in touch through letters.

14 September

We write each other frequently. He often tells me I'm strange. After one of the letters I wrote him he became moody, he thought I'd found another man, and then another letter arrives and his mood brightens. He continues to write that maybe this feeling is only because he loves me too much and is waiting for me to write him the way he writes me, and in closing, his last words are: "Write whatever you like, even if it isn't something personal, just write. Please write, so I have at least something from you!!"

Aside from these words, which I feel come straight from his heart, can I stop this correspondence with him the way they are telling me to? No! No, I can't. I'll keep lying just so he won't suffer.

Because no one suffers like he does. My brother is relieved because the letters are no longer coming here. I go to the post office to pick them up and he may think I still love him, which is true.

Today I wrote to him that he mustn't send letters to me anymore because I'm leaving Senta. As soon as I settle down some place permanent I'll write.

My uncle would like to take me to Zagreb, to Katica, my cousin. She would also like that, and my cousin Endre decided that all three of us would go to Zagreb. Gizika is getting ready to go to Budapest to her fiancé, and my brother is soon off to Belgrade to the consulate to get his paperwork in order.

Belgrade, 18 September

Yesterday we left Senta for Zagreb. My brother is with me. He went up to the American Embassy and we waited for him outside. We see him running, he comes down and gets into a jeep. We wait for three hours until he comes back, very pleased that they had hired him at the embassy to work for four months, and later he would be legally returning to his former major.

My brother stayed there and that same evening we continued on our way to Zagreb.

Zagreb, 23 September

I've written to Juro and already received his answer here in our new home. We're staying on the most beautiful street in Zagreb.

When I look out the window I feel as if I'm in Sweden, everywhere it's green and one villa after another. In the apartment we have a lot to do as we moved in yesterday. We've been staying at a hotel until they returned our apartment to us.

The apartment is filthy and we're cleaning it ourselves.

We have no furniture except in the kitchen, but our belongings, clothing, rugs, (Persian), bedding, silver—everything is ours. We had to borrow furniture, which we'll receive in another week.

30 September 1945

It's Hajnal's birthday. We celebrated it while celebrating the apartment move. Today we finally brought our new home into proper order. We've been sleeping on the floor on rugs, but now we have lovely furniture, and each has our own bed.

We've hardly even ventured into town except for this street and Vlaška, the next street over, where we do our shopping. Until now we've been so busy, but from now on we'll have more time.

WHAT ARE THE BLIND MEN DREAMING?

Noemi Jaffe

TRANSLATED FROM THE
BRAZILIAN PORTUGUESE BY
JULIA SANCHES

HISTORY

Some say it no longer makes sense to write about Nazism. Everything has already ostensibly been written, said, filmed, photographed, and examined, to the very limit. It would be ridiculous to want to extract even more possibilities of expression from an event that has been exhausted. The daughter once heard a story about the judge of a literary award who, when faced with a contestant who had written about the Holocaust, had claimed that the Holocaust "had seen its day," that it "had exhausted itself." Any reference to it could therefore be merely appellative; just another opportunity to explore a suffering that is continually proffering itself.

It has also been said that the Jews have benefited from a suffering that, on the one hand, was not only experienced by Jews and, on the other, has been and is being experienced to the same extent by many other ethnicities and in many other places, though it garners much less attention from the world and from the media. This is because Jews are more powerful, because they are in charge of more media outlets, show businesses, and because the examination of their suffering "sells more."

And it's true that everything has probably already been said and that saying more, or trying to say something else about the suffering of the Jews is to fall into a void, to explore a history whose meanings and lessons have all already been assimilated.

How can we respond to this kind of statement—that the Holocaust "has been exhausted"?

Maybe the Holocaust *has* been worn out and exhausted as a source of learning. At least, allegedly, in the collective sense. But not as an individual experience. It is impossible to tire of what was lived. An individual's past does not exhaust itself, nor should it. And, at the end of the day, the collective experience of war is no more than a collection of individual memories, and the collective study of war can only be political, while the suffering of each one of the prisoners and the survivors is not political and cannot be viewed politically, lest we run the risk of trivializing and exploiting their experiences.

But even then, what sense is there in telling yet another story of suffering?

This is just another story that will lose itself in the sea of survivors' stories, each one of them unique. There are no clear cut motives for telling this story. Both daughter's and mother's motives are uncertain, and yet they must be exposed: they are telling this story so that they might learn something, so that they might understand their memory and their forgetting, so that Mother's own micro-story might be inscribed onto the body of the world. These words can come to replace the memory she lost; not only because it is through them that it is told, but because these words can be used to anchor something whose natural tendency is to disappear. First of all, this book is an anchor for what Mother herself forgets. Secondly, for the daughter, this book is a token of what it is to try to be another person's memory, to be her mother's memory. Finally, this book is simply the daughter's attempt to better come to know her mother.

Nazism was conceived as a machine of extinction. The Nazi officers were cogs in this machine and had to act accordingly; and the Jews were the filth that had to be eliminated by this efficient machine, which had, in turn, to consistently prove its technical efficiency. The question of Nazism is a matter of technological competence; proof that a machine can work well. Like a dummy used to test the safety of a motor vehicle.

Hiroshima and Nagasaki were the same, in this sense: proof of the competence, or more accurately, the efficacy of a machine, of a technological device whose efficiency as a device could only be truly confirmed by launching it against its actual target—humans. And then there was the absurd political goal of allegedly ending the war and promoting peace. Even so, in practice, Nazism is still different, in that it requires time, the full collaboration of its people, ideology, and even idealism. The bomb is explosive, simultaneous, and does not require this extra component, a cooperative and collective ideology. With the bomb comes the discipline of destruction. Though this, of course, in no way minimizes the horror or the error of having launched it.

The singularity of Nazism—that it was an education in and for the extinction of humans—does not make it worse than the bomb or other historical genocides. Its specificity, however, does demand that people pay a different kind of attention to its meanings.

No matter how many survivors' stories there are, there will never be enough. Every and any account is welcome.

There are at most twenty years left until the last survivors disappear, until they die. When this happens, another stage in our history will begin. We must start preparing ourselves for it. Fifty years from now, will concentration camps be be no more than a name? Must history prepare itself for this? Will the word, *Auschwitz,* become like the word *Troy*, the word *Peloponnese*, the word *Manchuria?* If this—becoming a word—is the inevitable path of history, must those who live in the present count on its inevitability, today, and begin to trivialize things, before it happens, since it will happen anyway? The answer is no. The men and women of today are not the men and women of the future and they cannot and should not play the role that history might itself play. Let history do so however it sees fit. Those alive today must do nothing more than simply be who they are now: fallible in our need to repeat things again and again, but genuine in our need to want to tell it. We are not gods, nor realistic foretellers of time. We are ants, atrophied and lost, trying to find our way home.

THIRD PERSON

Since this story happened to her own mother and, in a way also to her, why does the daughter insist on writing in the third person?

The daughter doesn't want to explain, since she isn't quite sure herself. Perhaps it's that she doesn't feel comfortable telling this not-quite-story in the first person. None of this happened to her. She is only a voice, and wants to be no more than a voice. The third person, like the character of Dr. Pasavento in Vila-Matas's novel, is keen to disappear. Here, in this story, she clearly does not achieve this supreme and inestimable feat of disappearance, but she comes closer to it than she would have in the first person. The abstruse way in which she does appear here might even be more like the first person disguised as the third person, but it's the most this not-quite-author was able to achieve—to be the third person of herself and, especially, of her mother, who is the first person.

It is not for nothing that grammar designated the title of first person to "I." A person who doesn't possess the first person isn't able to articulate language, and therefore thought. Because of the way Western languages are built, everything inevitably ends in an "I"—for everyone. And so people believe that the world exists for the "I," which, fortunately, does not come remotely close to the full truth. The world doesn't exist for the I. It doesn't exist for anything. It exists to continue existing. But knowing this does not change a thing for all the I's who wander the world. The I of a woman in a burka shopping at a department store in London who coincidentally crosses paths with the I of an Indian cab driver who happens to be buying a watch there at the same time, and who crosses paths with a Brazilian woman who is also there buying anti-aging products, each with the certainty that at that moment the world revolves around them; the shock of simultaneity, of multiplicity, of dissociation, does not change, or perhaps only lightly alters, this sensation. The concept of the non-I also comes from the I. For thinking beings, the I is the infallible, the indubitable. The world cannot be thought from another perspective, lest the I end up also being dubitable, and there is no longer any certainty at all, and even the things we doubt turn out to be beyond doubt. To doubt the I that doubts is to open the door to the dogmatisms we are trying to combat. The I is the source of the certainty of our existence, but also of mad consumerism, which tries to fill that space, that pit of fear in each and every person.

Even so, in order for the I to be fully I, it must diligently dissociate itself from itself. This is not new, though the lack of novelty in no way minimizes the difficulty of doing so. It is very easy to turn this dissociation into simply another impersonation of the I-that-dissociates-itself-from-itself. The I is an artifice; it may be the best one we have, but it is an artifice nonetheless.

It would be brave for the daughter to once and for all adopt the I. To shoulder her voice and her identity, and to say that everything that is remembered and recounted here builds on this perspective. To shoulder all the advantages and disadvantages that come with this stance; the good and the bad parts of this account. To shed the stylistic burden that the third person brings, and to adopt the more genuine voice of a narrative.

The daughter is afraid to say I. This is her way of saying it.

FATE

When I arrived at the camp, I was wearing a blue checkered dress with a flared skirt. The German asked us to undress and made a mound of all our clothes. After delousing, we were told to grab, at random, a garment from that pile. I picked out precisely my blue checkered dress.

She believes wholeheartedly in fate. For her, as it is for all believers, fate is the force that predetermines those events that will occur in the lives of all living beings. Nothing is accidental. And if it were, she thinks, she'd be dead, and wouldn't have benefited from the many strokes of luck that had allowed her to survive. For her, fate is not necessarily God, but it could very well be; fate is perhaps more like a deity. She doesn't question the status of what she believes in, nor does she have any interest in discussing the matter. *Belief is not up to debate.*

The heroes of Greek tragedies challenged fate, and were punished for their acts of rebellion. Fate should be bowed to; not thought about, independently construed, or defied. It has been prescribed and will come to pass, for good or for ill. Fate is what happens; it is the place we travel to. What will pass will pass and we will travel where we will travel, even if the paths that lead there are unknown, unwanted, or tortuous.

Tragic heroes would dress themselves in goatskin, hence the name *tragedy*, from *tragos*, for goat. Their song, the *odia*, resembles the keening of a bovid who is in agony and for whom death is imminent; it is the intoxicated, Dionysian cry of one whose dying does not startle, because he is unconscious. It is the scapegoat that provokes catharsis, and the feelings of terror or compassion for the person whose guilt is being purged for defying what has fatally come to pass: fate. In this way, tragic spectators, now atoned and cleansed, leave the tragic play feeling cleaner, afraid to defy what comes to pass. Fate, fatality, fact. Fate is a fact and facts are not up for debate.

It's easy to understand why she believes in fate in such a sacred, untouchable way. As if her belief might help her atone for the fact that she survived, as if it could explain everything—the death of others, as well as her own survival. This faith would also have helped her build herself a fortress for her forgotten memories, which has allowed her to continue living in the best possible way. When everything is already written, it becomes easier to conceive of forgetting, or even surviving. Even so, it can't be an easy task. Remembering, or discrediting, fatality may sound painful and complex; attributing everything to strange, prescribed forces, is no easier. It is like the pain of a razor cut—the impossibility of glimpsing anything beyond the fact. It means renouncing the gesture and the memory of the past and the future; it is silence, impotence, surrender. It can be even harder than believing in nothing. *Sometimes I think I suffer more now than I did then because of what I went through; I was so innocent.*

To believe, though maybe the word here shouldn't be believe, but understand—to understand that the fact that she picked out the same dress was a coincidence, and not destiny, is easier, more beautiful, and more poetic. Coincidence is fate turned inside out; it is its exposed stitching. Coincidences are the charlatans that amble around within fate, continuously defying it without ever being punished.

Fate cannot reach them, they are too small. Coincidence also requires surrender and a certain amount of belief; we are always subject to it, no matter what we try to do. But coincidence also allows one a pause from action, or better, it allows people more freedom. Coincidences, when they occur, are also undeniable facts. The difference is that a coincidence could be another fact altogether, not necessarily the one that occurred. Which means that, in the realm of coincidence, when a fact is a fact, it is actually no more than a series of accidental circumstances. And so, finding one's own dress, coincidentally, becomes charged with a certain non-sense that is both beautiful in its possibility and in the shrewdness of the accidental. It is a mix of truth and lies. And so it starts to seem as if the dress could not have possibly had a flared skirt. Why would anyone go to a concentration camp in a flared skirt? And how could the skirt still be flared after such a long and tortuous journey? The flared skirt features in this story because of its dreamlike quality, because of the fabulistic nature of a story in which a mother finds her own dress.

There is so much in her story that is difficult to understand when thought of discreetly, and in detail. After disinfecting them, did the Germans simply allow the girls to dress in anyone's clothing? Why did they not all immediately get into their prison uniforms? Maybe she only wore that dress for a day; maybe she had to make herself a uniform out of the used dresses; and maybe this story took place in another situation altogether. None of this matters in the least. It's amazing that she found the dress, that it was checkered and blue, and that now she can't even really remember this story, as is the case with all the other stories.

The fact, or fate (or is fact fate?), is that this seems to be only one of the many coincidences and strokes of luck that she was privy to, and which symbolically announced a conspiracy of signs that would allow her to survive. (Luck is a string of coincidences manipulated by people who are lucky, and who collect and administer them in such a way that they continue acting in their favor.)

Why were some lucky while others weren't? Why were so few privy to happy coincidences? Were they chosen? No, surely not. This is a sordid thought for a person who is thinking about the war to consider. She herself accepts that fate played a hand in it all, but she will not comment on it, nor will she accept that she was chosen; it would be too presumptuous, she thinks. She doesn't know the why of it all; she simply accepts it. But she also thinks there must have been a reason. Maybe the only reason is the way in which each person knew how to and was able to manage these coincidences, so that they could take advantage of even the smallest of opportunities. Or maybe it's not that, either. So many canny people died, and she was always so innocent herself. They say that luck blesses the foolish, that those who don't expect it are the only ones it comes to. She expected nothing, but probably neither did anyone else.

GYPSY

A gypsy asked to read my palm. She said I would travel to a distant country and that I would have three daughters. I thought: this woman must be mad. I won't even make it to tomorrow.

She survived. And four years after the war ended, she arrived in a distant country where she went on to have three daughters. She's a bit of a gypsy herself, credulous, pure, and more Hungarian than Yugoslav. She doesn't have complex dreams involving metaphors of displacement and condensation; her dreams are much simpler, and she interprets them with certainty and ease. She dreams of bags of wheat; someone is pregnant. She dreams of a red dress for her eldest daughter's wedding; this daughter is later married in a red dress. And then there was the simplest yet most complex dream of all. Once, she dreamt she shoved her own feces down the toilet bowl with a broom. And she asked herself why she'd had this dream. She couldn't interpret it.

And so the camp gypsy leads us once again to the possibility of confabulation, and to the differences between fate and coincidence. How can we ask her not to believe in fate after a story like hers? And who was this gypsy? Her name was Linka, and she was approximately twenty-eight years old, from a town called Debrecen, in the depths of Hungary. She had lived out of caravans her whole life, and had witnessed many horrors, but nothing compared to what she was living through then. She had lost her father and her five brothers, and seemed about to disappear herself, she was so skinny and subdued. Even so, she offered to read mother's hands, as she did for many women when the war was nearing its end, when no one seemed to care what the future held for them. Hence the exactness of her prediction. From suffering and the lack of expectation comes the unique possibility to divine the future. The future is certain when it doesn't exist, when words are the greatest thing we can count on. In this case, the word creates the world. This explains the magical relationship she has with words, in Hungarian and Serbo-Croatian, as well as in Portuguese. She doesn't know these languages well, nor does she make much of an effort to master or to understand them. Her relationship with language belongs in part to a quasi-magical domain, as if words held power and a particular, autonomous existence she had yet to attain. She doesn't feel she can rise to where words live; she simply says what comes out of her mouth, with the fear that it may not be right. Which is why she says *kih* instead of *key*, *niddle* when she means *needle*, and *bootcher* for *butcher*. *The niddle*, the tool she's always worked with, was, amongst other things, what allowed her to make a living in Brazil. And in the same way that words hold a certain mystery to her, there is also a mystery in her relationship with cloth, with sewing and scissors, with marked up fabric, and with the women who worked at the factory and who all mastered their language without thought to the power of words. She continues to divine the future—more so than the past, which she has almost completely forgotten.

She has herself turned into Linka, the gypsy from Debrecen. Her Jewishness is a mixture of faith and superstition; a religion she has partly invented herself. For example, it is a Jewish custom for people to wash their hands after leaving a cemetery.

But she has decided that people must also wash their feet and so this has also become a family ritual. She has created another custom, too, which is to stop at a bakery on the way home from the cemetery, so as to dodge the angel of death who, according to her, has a habit of following people as they leave the cemetery. If she stops at a bakery, the angel of death will stay there and no one will die. In Pesach, during the telling of the story of the ten Egyptian plagues, the ritual requires that each person dab a drop of wine on their plate, one for each plague. She refuses to do this. She thinks this gesture, in its ostentatious declaration of hatred and vengeance toward Egyptians, is wrong. She refuses. In her world of superstitions, the cultivation of ill will or anger can only bring more future misfortune and, who knows, might even bring back the past misfortunes she has so efficiently managed to erase.

This is why the gypsy was able to get it right. Because she was reading the palm of a fellow diviner whose relationship with future facts and with the words that create them is one of respect, not mistrust or incredulity. Explanations aren't necessary, and perhaps not even belief or misbelief. It is enough just to know.

COLD

I don't know how we could stand the cold. These days, when I feel cold, I won't even leave the house. How could we live in such freezing temperatures and without any warm clothes? We can stand anything in life; I can hardly imagine how.

She says people pressed against each other at night to keep warm. Primo Levi also writes of how they collected paper, bits of old newspapers, and placards made of various materials, and put them underneath their uniforms to deaden the cold. The dictionary says that *aguentar*, to endure, bear, or withstand, in Portuguese is to grip a running rope; to hold the wind, like a sail. She always uses the word *aguentar*; it is part of her life repertoire. When someone says they have a problem and that nothing can be done about it, she always responds: *aguenta sim; a gente aguenta tudo; é só querer:* you can stand it; we can stand anything in life; all you have to do is want it. And, after all she's been through, no one can or will even try to question her. For men and women, who are not like the sails on a boat, endurance comes with a price. In her case, the circumstances made it so that she had no other choice. In other cases, other than those involving cold, hunger, or thirst, maybe it isn't necessary or even advisable to endure everything; maybe what we need is to resist less, to be a little weaker, so that the consequences of holding onto a running rope are not so severe. But not when it comes to the cold.

In the cold, you must hold on tight because the cold is a rope that runs mercilessly and those who live through it cannot but come out with souls that are drier, like when skin hardens and dries as it comes into contact with the cold air. But we forget about those freezing temperatures once winter has ended, and this is why she doesn't know, now, how she was able to stand it. But the cold left its secret, indelible marks. Because a person who has gone through intense, shelterless cold is necessarily different to a person who has never done so.

It was a harsh winter in Auschwitz in 2009. The snow was up to our knees and there was no heating in the barracks. We were well prepared and yet, even so, the cold was unbearable. There was the sound of people's labored breathing as they walked around, unable to stop and talk for even a couple of minutes without immediately shivering and shaking, words spoken with difficulty through teeth that clattered from the cold. They say that the winter of 1944 was one of the harshest on record in Europe. At times, it seemed as if nature itself were conspiring with the Nazis to ensure the most horrific of conditions. This, at least, must have been how they felt at the camp. That their extermination was orchestrated by divine, natural, and historic forces; that nothing could be counted on, because everything had turned against them. What could they hold onto? Only to the string of events, if anything at all.

We had blankets; we'd use hay straws to make needles and with a knife, we'd cut the blanket and then sew it into a dress. The German guard showed it off to everyone: "Look at what they did," she'd say. There is ingenuity even in the cold; brutal survival conditions lead people to acquire and to discover creative and unimaginable possibilities; even a German guard admires her capacity, and that of her cousins, with whom she shared everything, to improvise in the cold. The Nazis take away the possibility of survival and then admire the survivors who can handle it. It's like being surprised by a monkey who can do basic arithmetic. Except it's far worse than that. That must have been where she learned to sew. Not only did her ingenuity get her the Nazi guard's admiration, it also helped her survive in Brazil. She knew how to sew.

In the hallway of the small apartment they rented on rua José Paulino, where the rent was paid by father's family, she and her mother-in-law would spread out a piece of fabric, cut it, and sew it into kids' clothing. They would then pack it into a suitcase, which father would carry through the streets of Bom Retiro, Brás, and Mooca. Because he couldn't speak Portuguese, he clapped his hands and gestured at the clothes to get the attention of the people who lived in the neighborhood. He'd take naps underneath the trees and snack on the food she'd prepared for him. One day, an officer stopped him and took all his merchandise. To him, this was just a small example of the kind of persecution they had suffered. Why confiscate a street vendor's merchandise? Why the need to persecute, even in such benign circumstances? The German guard's approval of her ingenuity is as absurd as the Brazilian officer's decision to seize his merchandise. It is a form of revenge against the other's ability to deal with the impossible.

And it was with this, with sewing, that they were able to make their way in Brazil. This is how they endured. By sewing clothes for children, skirts for grown women, and all other kinds of clothes, for stores like Marisa and Hella and for the Middle Eastern merchants on 25 de Março, with whom Father eventually became close. He would miss walking along those streets once they opened a factory in Bom Retiro. Sometimes, he'd go back to Brás and to Mooca just so he could chat with the people on the street or in front of the shops. He'd talk with the sales clerks of Hella and Marisa, with the seamstresses, the drivers, the beggars, with the children who walked by on their way to or back from school, and the custodians. Meanwhile, she would stay at the factory, cutting large swathes of fabric, which she would then extend over a large wooden table. She'd mark them up and then cut the many layers of fabric all at once with a big machine, stacking the dozens of rolled up pieces at the front of the shop, where the kids would use them to play hide and seek. She continued sewing for a long time after she made that dress with the blanket they gave her in Auschwitz. These days, when it's cold out, she'll call to ask: *How are you handling the cold?*

HUNGER

In the beginning, we couldn't eat the bread because it tasted like sawdust. But later, when we were really hungry, we would hide the bread under our pillows so that no one could steal it. There were four of us and Gisie would split the bread in four so that we could eat one portion and leave the other three for later, because we were only given bread once a day. Gisie was the eldest and she was like the boss to the four of us: Alice, Helena, Gisie, and me.

For the hungry, it would seem that the need to eat is even stronger than the need to live. Yet there were few suicide cases in the concentration camps, even though this wouldn't have been difficult to accomplish. They would have had to do no more than throw themselves against the electric fence. But almost no one did—there was always the next piece of bread. Living reduced itself to eating; or more accurately, eating was worth more than living.

After the war had ended, when she was on her way to Sweden with the Red Cross, everyone offered her food. Chocolate, bread, candy. People threw food onto the train, happy to be able to feed those who had gone hungry. And even in the camp, the main topic of conversation was food, and many probably survived so they could remember food, talk about food, and eat food. They didn't eat to live; they lived to eat. Even in a situation of almost complete food deprivation, prisoners would constantly talk about it. *Sometimes I'd smile. We'd talk about food, and then we'd start remembering things: like how the dish was made, how we ate, you know that potato cake I used to make? And we'd go like this with our hands, do you remember?*

Knowing how to manage food—how to split it into portions, keep it, and bargain with it—turning bread into a currency, could guarantee you one more day, one more day to find one more piece of bread. This paltry maintenance of the body and of what was left of their minds allowed prisoners to talk at night, during work hours, or simply in conversation, about other, more sophisticated foods, to gesticulate about it and make believe it existed.

Dreams, it seems, were also filled with food. The body and the soul of a person who starves are full of the constant demand for food. (What soul? What is the soul of a starved prisoner, of any starved person? Hunger can make a person feel like the soul is an invention of the body, by and for those who are well-fed and do not have to think about food.) As if humans had become parasites, crazed bacteria, spinning unnecessarily in a void, desperately seeking crumbs—not in order to live, but to eat. Eating to eat. This process of animalization reinforced the Nazis' perception that the prisoners were indeed animals, which in turn reinforced their hatred of them and justified their persecution. Wouldn't it have been more dignified, then, to commit suicide? Why suffer such humiliation for a piece of old, hardened bread? People would steal bread from each other, from corpses. But why? Many Israelis resent the prisoner for not resisting more, for submitting with such mildness, like animals, and for only a ration of soup and a piece of bread. There is both an inversion and perversion in these ideas. No one who is not now starving or has once starved can understand what it means to do so, or the effects it has on a person's behavior, no matter how ethical that person may be. No one knows whether life, or, even more absurdly, a person's values, can be more important than eating when there is no food.

The Nazis' strategy was to transform the effects of complete deprivation—hunger, thirst, filth—into their cause. What was happening to the Jews was happening because they had always been animals, not because they'd been turned into animals. This is the basis of any process of alienation: to switch cause and effect. And the other people, those who were not Nazis and who criticize the prisoners, make the same mistake. They take pleasure in judging and in asking questions, which is something only someone who has food can do. Few recognize the strength needed to endure humiliation, to search for ways to manage one's hunger, to become an insect, with a small voice deep within the little life there is left that insists that the human within you lives on. Dignity is not inflexible.

In the pages of her diary, as it is in the diaries of many other survivors, there is a lot about food. A turnip, an apple, potato peels, half a ration of frozen and contaminated soup, a bit of butter. Each one of these is a reason to live another day; life, under these conditions, is no more than one day at a time. She talks about eating rotten potatoes, and laughs. *We'd eat rotten potatoes like they were made of gold! I'd never eaten something so delicious. You know, when you're starving, everything tastes good!* Maybe this is why she often made a game out of food when her children were young. She diced sausages into squares and put them on little circles of black bread, which were held in place with tooth picks. These, she would call "little soldiers." She would make chicken and set it in the center of the plate, surround it with rice, and drizzle white sauce around the edges. She would call this "the island."

There was the leftover dough from the jelly-filled potato cakes, which she'd cut into strips and call "little snakes." There was spinach and eggs, peach soup with egg whites whipped to a peak, and coffee ice cream cannoli. Then there was the goulash and cholent that she'd spend all night preparing, waking up twice in the night to stir it; a mixture of meat, eggs, potato, and white beans. Food for those who had nothing to eat and who, by mixing everything together, had come up with a dish that went on to become part of the national cuisine. Sirloin steak on the grill, fried only in butter. And Friday night dinners with grandma and her brother, Uncle Artur. Elaborate dinners, with a starter, a main, and dessert. She was never extravagant in the kitchen, and she didn't know many recipes, but the ones she did know, she had mastered. And then there were the Yom Kippur cakes, chocolate cake rolls, drizzled with warm chocolate sauce, walnut cake rolls, and spaghetti kugel.

Mother seems to enjoy watching others eat more than she herself enjoys eating. She eats so little, and has never liked restaurants, where she always insists on sharing, and refuses to order individual dishes. The daughter thinks it is strange that the smaller the dish, the more expensive it is. Odd that it is elegant to eat little and that skeletal thinness is a sign of beauty, that eating too much is for the poor. To what extent is this steady emaciation, and the individualization of food connected to the horror of the Holocaust? Why are the economically affluent attracted to minimalism? Perhaps it's a way of directly challenging the uncontainable desire to have more by those who are materially deprived. In any case, baroque abundance is also offensive, though more sincere and less refined. In order to eat well, must men always remember those who eat little and poorly? Do those who starved have more of a right to ritualize food than those who didn't? No. The memory of hunger should not deprive those who can eat. The ethical relationship between past and present hunger should not be mathematical, direct—that would be ridiculous—as if one's eating less would make another eat more. No, this is just another way of avoiding the issue. Our respect for those who did not eat should not be demonstrated by not eating. Eating well and ritualizing the practice of food is a way of engaging with the earth and the other.

Beyond the use of direct assassinations, the Nazis' strategy of annihilation and radical extermination consisted entirely in producing hunger. Hunger is the worst kind of privation, the most beastly of them all, and it is hunger that sustained this paranoid extermination of the prisoners' cultural and human identities. It wasn't only that it was materially and logistically difficult to send people to the gas chambers, hunger was also a necessary step in the process of diminishing man's humanity. Concentration camps are hunger, and hunger is, more than anything, the determining factor of all other occurrences.

STONE

One of my cousins stole margarine from the kitchen, and the guards suspected her of doing it. I'd gone to visit a friend in another barrack. When I came back, my cousins asked me to turn myself in and to tell the guards that I was the thief. I had nothing to lose so I went over and told them it was me. The guard said he'd kill me, but I said I was very sorry and so he decided that he would only punish me. I spent a whole day on my knees, on the gravel, holding an enormous stone over my head.

It's impossible to dramatize the stone, to turn it into a metaphor. Yet, even so, this event, this fact, is what is most present in her own memory and in her daughters' memories, as if the stone synthesized Mother and the war—even though it also doesn't. There is no way to synthesize war. Nothing can symbolize war or suffering, even if the object-stone, the object-punishment, and the object-butter could all somehow be turned into symbols. No one outside this history has the right to turn it into a story. But then, how does something become a story? How do we tell facts? And, how can we listen to this fact?

In 2009, in Auschwitz, this stone could have been in any and every corner of the camp, and the place where she held the stone could have been any place. And, yet, this place and this stone would never be there because what happened, even if it once happened in a specific place, was no longer there. If fate is what will fatally come to pass, then the past is what has fatally passed, which is why it can be forgotten by those who lived it. The duty to remember rests only with those who haven't lived it; and yet, there is no hope of them being able to do so, because it—the thing that must be remembered—is gone. To try, again, to see the place where it all happened and, once there, to also clearly see the stone that was held, or the place where she held it is an endeavor so poetic that it borders on the ridiculous.

It's difficult to understand why people feel the need to visit Auschwitz, a visit which shouldn't be emotional, but rather documentary and informative—though this seems impossible. Seeing, being there, picturing the place where she held that stone—it chills the soul forever. She never wants to go back. She doesn't want to watch films about the war, read books about the war, or even listen to people talking about it. This all seems justified, and yet, somehow, when you look at her, the stone is still there. To know that she held a stone over her head for a whole day, injuring her knee forever, because her cousin had stolen some butter, can't help but provoke a permanent gravitational pull, or downward tug, in the memories of those who listen to this story and in the memories of her daughters, like an anchor that is slowly and constantly sinking a little more every day, a little more with every dream.

And, yet, the stone should not be overestimated, made into an icon, or used as a further motive for one to feel shocked, or to suffer, if she will not do so herself. What right do other people have to suffer more than she does? To "over-suffer," "alter-suffer," to suffer over the dehumanization she did not actually feel because the war was, for her, a matter of fact where, for others, it is so much more than that. This can, at times, leave the impression that compassion—the idea that a person can fully feel the pain of another—is a sham because there is no way to suffer in the place of another, no way to truly empathize. The compassionate understand pain, but pain cannot be understood. Those who suffer understand nothing.

So, what is the moral of the stone? What sense is there in knowing this harrowing story? Maybe the sense is in knowing that there is no sense to it, and that nothing can be learned from it. She cannot, cannot, *cannot* be turned into a heroine because of how horrifically she suffered, no matter how tempting it may be. Suffering was commonplace in the camp and her punishment was moderate and bearable. And yet, it's so difficult to look at her at length and not picture her holding that stone. And if she's forgotten everything, how does this everything now determine who she is? Or was it the stone, amongst many other things, that determined her decision (or her non-decision, it's impossible to determine) to forget? She has forgotten and no longer thinks about it, but if someone asks her and if she does decide to talk, what she talks about is the stone.

And why did the guard give her a lesser punishment and not send her instead to the gas chamber? Why did she decide to pay for an act she did not commit? Why did her cousins ask her to? Perhaps she felt indebted to them because they had helped her get work in the kitchen, which had saved her life. In a previous roll call, her three cousins had been chosen to work in the kitchen, but she hadn't. The following day, her cousins had insisted she line up again for the roll call and, this time, she had been chosen. The commandant had noticed there was an extra prisoner in line, and so she pulled someone else out, someone who may have died because of what she did.

Maybe she felt indebted to her cousins and also to the other woman who died in her place.

The stone-as-fact is larger than the stone-as-history, than the stone-as-symbol. But those who have not experienced the stone itself, and who are sons and daughters of the fact, can only think of it as an indirect occurrence which carries symbolic force.

stone:
shulamite stone, Margareta stone, square stone, rectangular stone, cement stone, sand stone, pointy stone, smooth stone, heavy stone, dense stone, large stone, practical stone, brittle stone, gray stone, opaque stone, real stone, unreal stone, painful stone, still stone, movable stone, difficult stone, impassable stone, hard stone, hardy stone, lost stone, equal stone, common stone, unique stone, idiotic stone, innocent stone, sticky stone, distant stone, actual stone, crusty stone, loose stone, any stone, mineral stone, ornamental stone, stony stone, polished stone, touchstone, philosopher's stone, fundamental stone, chipped stone, sleek stone, a stone in your shoe, precious stone, semi-precious stone, rolling stone, kidney stone, keystone, crumbling stone, sharpening stone, dry stone, pre-stone, post-stone, to throw the first stone, to squeeze blood from a stone, to be hard as stone, to never have seen the stone, to picture the stone, to be in her place, holding the stone

Being the child of a survivor means feeling the temptation, in some distant and inhospitable part of your memory, to have been in the survivor's place. To not have let her live through all that she lived through, to travel to the past and stop him, to kill the guard who ordered her punishment. To pierce through time and through the camp's regulations, and save her. A mother who has suffered is a failure of history, a twisted reversal, which leaves her children with a minute guilt, an absence, and a dream or a nightmare that they carry with them throughout the day, and which both impedes and stimulates life. The desire to save one's mother is also a desire to eradicate her suffering from all our memories so that she herself can be freed of it, so that she can live without the stone.

ANGER

The skin on my knees was all torn up after I held the stone. The Germans called another roll call and, this time, Mengele was the one who was going to examine us. I was so scared. He was very precise. I was naked, but I held my clothes in front of my knees so he couldn't see them. I looked healthy and, luckily, he didn't see my knees and let me pass.

Mengele, known as The Angel of Death, died in Bertioga, Brazil in 1979. They say he experimented with rats, inserting them into the bellies of pregnant women, and that he injected people with poison, and turned people into soap. A man once recognized his own friend in a lampshade because on it he had seen his friend's tattoo. This man-myth of Nazi sadism examined her and then let her pass; maybe he thought he'd let a pretty face slide; maybe he was distracted at the exact moment he walked past her; or maybe he was preoccupied with something else altogether. She must have also been seen, commanded, and examined by other comparable monsters, but none like Mengele who, later, lived and died so near her.

I'm not angry at anyone. Not even at the Nazis. I don't like being angry. This suppression of anger must also be part of the surgical process of forgetting. Feeling anger means feeding the memory of facts and stories so that they (memory and anger) can be continuously maintained, so that they may be retraced, and become a legacy for the following generation. All her daughters find it difficult, as she does, to be angry. Her preference is always to silence a fight, whether big or small. When asked about an opposing view, a difference of opinion, or a disagreement, she prefers to say: *It doesn't matter, let's talk about something else.* When witnessing a misunderstanding, she will try to appease the differences with a *forget about it, it doesn't matter.* If one of her daughters speaks ill of the other, she will conceal their gossip, and even change its content. And if two of her daughters are fighting, she will ask them to make peace, buy presents for them and say to both that the gift was from her sister. When she argued with her husband, even though he was ostensibly guilty, she was always the one who, after a little while, would apologize.

Where is her anger? It must be somewhere. Perhaps it is a compressed anger that exists in a state of the highest-purified concentration. Or perhaps it is everywhere, hidden in plain sight, it progresses millimetrically like a bee or an almost imperceptible spider who gradually and carefully build their homes. It acts like a thread, a veil, but is there, nonetheless, both in her forgetting and in her reconciliation.

Reconciliation at any cost is also one of the manifestations of anger, it is a refined vengeance. Her daughters also suffer from it. How difficult it is to simply hate! To say what we think, to spit out our anger and say *I don't want it, don't like it, won't go there.* The suppression of anger creates a personality prone to concession and accommodation, which can be easily mistaken for an innate generosity. Perhaps all great acts of generosity conceal great anger. Are her daughters angry because she isn't? Primo Levi feels anger, Elie Wiesel feels anger, Ruth Klüger feels anger, Jorge Semprún feels anger. To remember, we must feel anger; and to feel peace, we must forget. "Never shall I forget that night, the first night in camp, that turned my life into one long night seven times sealed... Never shall I forget those flames that consumed my faith forever," vowed Elie Wiesel.

Jacques le Goff writes that "to be Jewish is to remember." But how can we keep our faith and our memories if both are irreconcilable? To say that God does unknowable things may sound hypocritical to us now, and yet there were many religious men and women in the camps. Primo Levi wrote about a Lithuanian rabbi who, on a day of fasting, would not eat his soup and asked that the commandant save it so that he could eat it the next day. In the thirty years the commandant had served in the German army, he had never seen a prisoner refuse food. The rabbi's faith so impressed him that he saved him an even larger portion of the soup for the next day.

How can we continue believing after such suffering? Or is it suffering itself that leads some to believe more fervently? To believe, to feel rage, to remember, to forget; there is no correct answer. Mengele probably also believed in something. What kind of God can exist for both her and for Mengele? David Grossman wrote of how he could no longer bring himself to speak a language in which one could articulate the words "I killed your Jew" as expressed by the Nazi solider who killed Bruno Schulz. And so he resolved to speak another language, the language of literature, the mad language, the false language, the only language in which you can switch up tenses and place feminine articles before masculine nouns. As in *you the blond woman was the clouds that race before my your his our yours their faces. What the hell.*

The opposite of literary language is that of a concentration camp—there is no language more organized or more orderly. There, language was at its most refined and standardized, at its most efficient for communication. There, grammar was not kidnapped, nor experimented with or twisted. It was correct and perfect; with it evil could be skillfully and expertly perpetrated. The German language—monosyllabic, overpopulated with consonants, commutatively flexible, in which any two words can be joined to form a new one—seems as if it could serve any purpose. In her daughter's dreams, as a teenager, and also later, in 2009 in Germany, the word, *schnell*—quick—fulfilled its mythical and ideological role. *Schnell*, a word that had haunted her adolescent memories and terrorized her dreams, which reminded her of those soldiers who had yelled orders at her mother, with the command, "S*chnell, schnell*," inflicting on the prisoners the demand for an impossible rhythm, was there, in Germany, in real life, where people will say *schnell* everywhere and at any time. *Schnell* is a bellicose word.

Her trip to Germany in 2009 was interspersed with the active reinterpretation and review of all the words she read on the streets. The monosyllabic nature of the language made it seem petrified to her, which suits the story of her mother holding a stone over her head. *Geld* for money. Gold, the thing and not the money, a diluted derivation of silver. *Trinkt* to drink; *essen* to eat; *nicht* for no. It seemed so much easier in her mind to disobey a Portuguese no, *não*, a sweeter word and almost as beautiful as *sim*, yes. But the disobedience of *nicht* rings of condemnation. On the other hand, *yes* in German is *ja*, which sounds obedient—not generous, loving, or trusting. A German *yes* is an inverted *no*. And in Poland, the meeting of consonants is even greater, which can't help but provoke in the visitor a sense of the impossibility of belonging. While walking through Warsaw in 2009, after various failed attempts to find information about a certain street, a sign finally came into view: *droga wewnętrzna*, which means *dead end*, or something similar. It is as if the language itself conspired to make a person feel disoriented and alone. By translating a sense of abandonment, it affirmed that nothing and no one, not a single word, would help.

And even so, Paul Celan and Bruno Schulz both wrote chaotically in German. It was in the language of the speakable, in its most acute state, that Celan was able to express the unspeakable:

> *Black milk of morning we drink you at dusktime*
> *we drink you at noontime and dawntime we drink you at night*
> *we drink and drink*
> *we scoop out a grave in the sky where it's roomy to lie*
> *There's a man in this house who cultivates snakes and who writes*
> *who writes when it's nightfall* nach Deutschland *your golden hair Margareta*
> *he writes it and walks from the house and the stars all start flashing he whistles his*
> *dogs to draw near*
> *whistles his Jews to appear starts us scooping a grave out of sand*
> *he commands us to play for the dance*
>
> *Black milk of morning we drink you at night*
> *we drink you at dawntime and noontime we drink you at*

dusktime
we drink and drink
There's a man in this house who cultivates snakes and who
writes
who writes when it's nightfall nach Deutschland *your golden*
hair Margareta
your ashen hair Shulamite we scoop out a grave in the sky where
it's roomy to lie
He calls jab it deep in the soil you lot there you other men sing
and play
he tugs at the sword in his belt he swings it his eyes are blue
jab your spades deeper you men you other men you others play
up again for the dance

Black milk of morning we drink you at night
we drink you at noontime and dawntime we drink you at
dusktime
we drink and drink
there's a man in this house your golden hair Margareta
your ashen hair Shulamite he cultivates snakes

He calls play that death thing more sweetly Death is a gang-boss
aus Deutschland
he calls scrape that fiddle more darkly then hover like smoke
in the air
then scoop out a grave in the clouds where it's roomy to lie

Black milk of morning we drink you at night
we drink you at noontime Death is a gang-boss aus Deutschland
we drink you at dusktime and dawntime we drink and drink
Death is a gang-boss aus Deutschland *his eye is blue*
he shoots you with leaden bullets his aim is true
there's a man in this house your golden hair Margareta
he sets his dogs on our trail he gives us a grave in the sky
he cultivates snakes and he dreams Death is a gang-boss aus
Deutschland

your golden hair Margareta
your ashen hair Shulamite

In this language of order, it is also possible to sow disorder, under the auspices of language itself. The sense of those same words that were used to empty the world—because their combinations of sound and sense were so perfect and so well-suited to the purpose they were destined for—when repeated poetically (*we drink, we drink, we drink; He calls: Death is a gang-boss* aus Deutschland), become shriller and shriller until they are turned into crutches for the devil, absurd speak, the voice itself of the inaudible. Celan maximally disorganizes language by using the fact itself that German is the apex of order. *Death is a gang-boss* aus Deutschland; and all serve the gang-boss, Nazis and Jews alike. And, in the camp, what can be seen after sixty years of active, perpetrated death, when all that is left of it are its shadows, is death under the terrifying language of order. It was order that built and also destroyed the war. In the camps, it becomes clear how madly organized the

Germans were, leaving behind traces of absolutely everything they did: how many gold teeth they had torn out of mouths each day, how much money they had collected through theft, how much hair had been gathered to send to the rope factory. Every aspect of the Death-gang-boss routine was meticulously noted, as if it had never occurred to them that they might lose the war. And, after they had lost, the criminals themselves left behind traces of their crimes, like trophies or sacrificial alters to Mother Death. What can be seen in every corner of the camp, apart from the shadow of death, is order, which is another form of death, or, more precisely, the language itself of death.

Maybe it's because of this, though perhaps indirectly, that she and her daughters strive for a level of disorderliness that borders on the infantile. They boast of a proud and deliberate resistance to order and a delight in mess, as if this were payment for their mother's suffering, a revenge against German order itself. Order, bureaucracy, is a means that does not lead to an end, a means that serves only itself. It's a language that spins on its own axis, drawing in people, institutions, values, and possibilities; an infinite mediation, which feeds itself and creates the illusion of content when, in truth, it is no more than the demand for its eventuality. It is a language without meaning, no more than an empty signifier.

DIGNITY

One night, we had to sleep in the sawdust. I knew it would be teeming with lice, so I undressed, folded my clothes and slept naked. That way the lice wouldn't infest my clothing.

Does having a sense of dignity help a person survive? It would seem so. Primo Levi wrote of *musselmen*, Jewish men and women who were so bowed, so inert and apathetic, that their posture resembled that of a Muslim in prayer. They say the *musselmen* were the first to die; people for whom everything had lost sense, who would not raise their heads even an inch, or heal their wounds. But then, who was able to keep their dignity? How did some keep it while others did not? Is it that they had more energy, more fat reserves? Because they'd had a more stable upbringing? Because they were stronger, more ignorant and, therefore, felt less humiliated when they were made to obey ridiculous orders? Were women, who were much more used to restrictions and more familiar with personal hygiene, better than men at keeping their dignity? How was she able to think of it all so meticulously, to the point of considering how the lice might infest her clothing, having the patience and disposition to sleep naked and, most impressively of all, taking the care to fold her clothes? Primo Levi also writes of those workers who, despite the banality of their work—for example, erecting useless walls—would still take pains to build them efficiently, and with rigor, refusing to cheat the Germans. Why work so efficiently? And why fold one's clothes? Was it perhaps because of an innate sense of dignity, or was it in order to impress the Germans, if only a little? And if so, do prisoners of war still hold the illusion that it's possible to please their executioner? That keeping one's dignity will make one less of an animal in the eyes of the enemy, and more of an individual? In wartime, is the desire to be an individual humiliating? Or is it a matter of an automatic impulse, a habit, or the result of the individual's belief that they are still individuals capable of folding clothes and working efficiently? As always, the border between the highest egotism and the highest altruism is muddled. And perhaps even more in a situation such as hers.

To brush one's teeth, avoid lice, wash one's face, shave, shower, mend clothes, mend shoes, make the bed, clean the floor, find something that can be used as a broom, dust, look oneself in a mirror, eat with a spoon, make sure to clean the urine and feces off one's body; do all these things keep a person alive? Is this what, under any and every circumstance, will keep a person alive?

The etymological dictionary posits that *dignity* comes from worthiness, as in "to be worthy of." And if that's so, dignity, which we now understand to be a sense of self-esteem, of pride in one's personality, and of the preservation of a certain nobleness of character, actually has its origins in the ability of an individual of inferior standing to do justice to the position of inferiority he feels he deserves. Like a soldier who will tie his laces and iron his shirt collar when he knows the commandant is going to stop by. The soldier who keeps his laces tied is worthy of continuing as a soldier and might even be promoted to a slightly higher post. Dignity is, in other words, the ability to accept one's inferiority. Dignity is obedience. And this is when things become confusing.

Those who are able to preserve the slightest sense of dignity might actually be doing nothing more than obeying a general desire for order; while those who give in, who are weak, and who fly off the handle, in turn, are brave, they are resisters. This is why Camus saw resistance in Sisyphus; he resists destiny by accepting the pointlessness of his task. And that is also why there is a certain heroism in a person letting herself be taken to the gas chambers without resisting. Not because it would have been useless to do so, but because not resisting might be the bravest form of resistance.

She never made much of an effort to teach her daughters the basics of hygiene and self-care. They never learned that you should wash your hands before eating, brush your teeth at night, or fold and iron your clothes. Maybe it was because she didn't think these things had to be taught, that they were innate. To her, these tasks were either so necessary that you just learned them without trying, or, on the other hand, they were of so little importance that they needn't even be carried out. In any case, she educated her daughters liberally, at least compared to other mothers, like those Brazilian mothers who were always much more concerned with their daughters' hygiene and whether they went out late at night, with money, and grades.

She never knew their grades. She only knew if they had failed; that was all that mattered. She never knew of their successes. Anything was good enough. She barely ever glanced at their report cards—that was the father's responsibility. She gave her daughters money when they asked for it and let them do whatever they wanted: travel, go out, date, and play with whoever they wanted to play with. She never controlled them. Even after going through everything she went through (or maybe precisely because of this), she was not demanding, nor worried too much about her daughters. She gave them almost complete freedom. And the little she did ask for was more so to satisfy their father, who thought that the way she educated their daughters was negligent.

She never talked to them about menstruation, nor about sex. They found all that out on their own, and they felt a mixture of timidity, awkwardness, lack of preparation. But they also held the belief that people learn things independently and that it isn't necessary for someone to tell them how, to teach them, and to repeat it over and over. People just learn.

When a person lives through a war, all their future attitudes are automatically justified. If the person is extremely neurotic, traumatized, or haunted, it is justified. Also if he or she is resentful, whiny, weepy. Or if, like Mother, they become inattentive, withdrawn, forgetful, bordering on negligent.

One night, in the 1970s, the house on rua Bandeirantes caught fire. A neighbor in the building was able to put it out. After this, Mother went to play cards with her friends. Her husband and their youngest daughter stayed at the apartment to clean up the water and the foam, and to rescue the little furniture that had survived. Her husband cried while he mopped up the water. *How can she go play* buraco *at a time like this?* When telling this story, the response is always inevitably the same—that she feels the need to instantly forget tragedy.

It's difficult to assimilate this interpretation. And perhaps what's most difficult of all is to accept that she is made up of what she has forgotten; that this axis constitutes her personality.

It's hard to accept that everything might be justified by war. Yet, on the other hand, it *is* justified. How can we divine the morals of a person who has survived a concentration camp? What moral demands can we make on survivors? None? Can we insist that she remember, not the place itself, but other problems she later encountered? Can we accept that she has created an internal, automatic procedure by which she forgets all her problems? Everything she has forgotten can be attributed to this, to a mechanism that is associated with the war that, acting chemically, or psychologically, saws off memory with a blunt knife, and throws a Margareta stone on the memory? Is memory the master of death?

And who are the children of this forgetting? Should they remember? Can they help it? Are they also condemned to forget?

FAMILY

When we arrived at the camp, my mother had been trying to hide her two nephews under her coat. Her sister had gone mad on the journey there. The Germans sent those who would survive to the left and those who would die to the right. My mother and father went right. I never saw them again.

She can't help wondering had her mother not tried to protect her nephews, would she have been safe? Should she not have protected them, since it was obvious they would hurt her chances? Of course, Mother also says that it was all for the best, that it was the hand of fate. If her mother had not died that way, she would have died some other way and, who knows, maybe she would have suffered more. She speaks affectionately of her mother. She talks about how, as a child, she'd help out in the kitchen counting eggs—one, two, three, *crack*, one, two, three, *crack*—and cracking every third egg. Her mother would see this and laugh. Then there was the time when, in the middle of the night, her mother got some bad news and hurried out of the house without a coat, through the snow, to help someone who was sick. Because of this, she caught pneumonia and almost died.

She sings a song in Hungarian, which was also spoken in her hometown, Senta, along with Serbo-Croatian: *Erwi, Lili, Shari, Marishka, Rosali, Ella, Bella, Iutchi, Karolina, Gerte Otche Razno.* In the song, a mother calls her eight daughters to dinner. These eight daughters are her family and the mother who is calling them is her own mother. The mother in the song who calls her eight daughters is all mothers calling their daughters to dinner.

Mothers call their daughters to dinner and the daughters go eat dinner. This, independent of women's history and of feminism, is what it means to be a mother—to call one's daughters to dinner. And this, going to eat dinner, is what it means to be a daughter. Just like the woman in the song, she also has only daughters. Her three daughters are also those eight daughters. She did not know how to, was not able to, and did not want to be a mother who would keep calling her daughters to dinner, and they did not know how to, were not able to, and did not even want to be the kinds of daughter who went to dinner. But none of this matters, because at the end of the day, that is what she did, that is what she is. She is a mother who makes goulash, Pesach and Rosh Hashanah dinner, and her daughters go to her with their families.

Her three daughters are great hostesses, love having guests over, and serving them food. In their family, there is an eagerness to serve which could even be construed as feminist because of how it maintains a certain femininity, and in its subtle, yet inexorable, command of domesticity. Father would always say: *The best marriages are those in which the husband loves his wife more than she loves him. The wife must be able to exert her command over the husband without him realizing. He has to believe he is in charge.* This is all very sexist and she is even a bit sexist herself. But, seen from another angle— a slanted, subterranean angle—there is a certain non-sexism in this, too; perhaps one that only her and her daughters can understand. There might even be a feeling of feminine superiority in this fake sexism; a female lineage that can be traced to her mother, to the woman who protected her nephews.

Her brother, who had been with her and her parents, was also sent to the left, with the survivors. Even so, she didn't see him at the camp. In 1946, after the end of the war, she returned to her hometown to see whether any of her family members had survived and learned that her brother had escaped from one of the camps and joined an American military detachment, later falling in love with a 14-year-old girl. He gave the girl his sister's identity papers, which she used to go to the United States. They left her on her own in Yugoslavia, with no means of identification.

Her sister-in-law took her name and her brother betrayed her. Yet despite this, she wanted to go to the United States, to join him there. She was married so she could go to Brazil, and from there, travel north. But she didn't. And she never took care to maintain her relationship with her brother. He came to Brazil once, in 1969, and she visited him in the United States in 1959, then in 1971, and three more times after that. He owned a furniture factory, was very rich, and lived in a very big house in Detroit. After many years, he lost everything and fell ill and then, after many more years in which he didn't speak with her, he died.

She called to say: *My brother died.* It was as simple as that; the only person who had lived through everything she had lived through, who knew everything she knew, had died. Her three cousins had also died. She'd visited them, but none of them had ever felt the need or taken the care to try to remember what they had lived. They died. He died. What happened, happened. She resents them as much as she does him, but not because of what they did or of what he did during the war, and not even because he gave her identity papers to his girlfriend. It was because of how they acted afterward. It also isn't because they did not want to remember—they're just like her in that way. It's because they never tried to visit her or asked how she was doing in Brazil.

Strength of will is, to her, of the greatest importance—as if it could determine and control everything: pain, sickness, problems, misfortunes. Strength of will is even greater than fate and, who knows, might even have a hand in directing it. Likewise, to her, weakness is unforgivable. She won't forgive those who sink under the weight of their problems, who waver, who cannot stand pain. In a way, this condemnation of weakness compensates for her capacity to forget; as if it were her way of remembering. Her authority, as one who has withstood atrocious and unspeakable suffering, allows her to hate weakness. It is obvious from the way she acts—delicate only to those who really know her, like her daughters—that she is still a bit superstitious when it comes to weakness of character or—and this is more complicated, more painful—happiness and pleasure. If someone close to her insists on expressing excessive suffering for a loss or because they feel pain, she freezes up—as if she were controlled by an external force that conclusively forbids her from sympathizing. There is in this a combination of the disapproval she feels of another's suffering and the fear of mixing with it, of letting herself be contaminated. And so she just leans in and whispers: *Aguenta*. And the size of this word, independently of whatever subterranean substance it might contain, is able to exterminate, or at least lessen this pain.

Likewise, when one of her daughters shares with her a great pleasure, or joy, or pride for an achievement, she holds back, contains herself. If her daughter praises her own son: *He's so beautiful, isn't he?* she stays silent, as if to say: *It's not wise to praise so much.*

Much less to self-praise—it can bring bad energy and summon up bad luck. It's not good to toy with luck like that, to boast about one's happiness and to feel pride in one's pleasure. Bad luck lingers. All of which demonstrates that, in her own way, she hasn't forgotten. That she is always remembering. Her forgetting is part of her strength of will; it is her way of pushing the feces deeper into the toilet. She forgets because she can't bear it, because she fears remembering, superstitiously. And because she has pushed her memories to the back of her mind, her memory is gone and instead manifests itself in other ways. In an unbreakable strength of will, in superstition, and impenetrability.

In 2001, when the planes flew into the World Trade Center, she called her daughter and exclaimed: *Help, do something, it'll start all over again! They're jumping, they're killing themselves!* Her daughter had never heard her speak like that, and she actually isn't even sure it really happened at all. She knows her mother called her in the heat of the moment as she watched people jumping out of the buildings, but she isn't absolutely certain that this is what she said, even though she somehow has the memory of it. Does her mother remember saying this over the phone? Will her daughter have to protect her from another experience like the one she has already lived through, and which might eventually happen again?

What her daughter fears more than anything in the world is that her children might have to live through a war, that they might go hungry. She fears that a war will separate them. That a government, a cause, or a collective purpose could take on a force so violent it would separate a mother from her child. That someone might think it just, that this separation might be justified.

MOTHER

Mother.

In German: *Mutter*; in Armenian: *mayr*; in Bulgarian: *maĭka*; in Catalan: *mare*; in Chinese: *mŭqīn*; in Haitian Creole: *manman*; in Danish: *mor*; in Spanish: *madre*; in Estonian: *ema*; in French: *mère*; in Greek: *mitéra*; in Hebrew: *ima*; in Hindi: *maa*; in Portuguese: *mãe*; in Icelandic: *móðir*; in Latin: *mater*; in Maltese: *omm*; in Romanian: *mamă*; in Swahili: *mama*; in Thai: *Mǽ*; in Vietnamese: *mẹ*.

In most of the world's languages, *M* is either the first letter or main sound in the word "mother"; that is, except in Arabic, Indonesian, Malaysian, Finnish, and a handful of others. You can pronounce an *m* continuously, uninterruptedly, with your mouth closed, using practically only your throat and nose; it is an easy sound to make, even for a small baby. It also resembles a baby's cry, a prolonged *ñ* or a drawn-out *n*. While suckling, the baby's grumblings resemble a *mmm*, perhaps because of the proximity of sleep, because they are sated and satisfied, or maybe because they want more. When babies really want something they also say *mmm, hmmm, hãamm*. *M*s are in the smack of a kiss, in the onomatopoeic *yum*. *M*, it seems, is a primary sound, though there is also *dah, tah, pah*. But mothers have *m*. Mothers are eaten, wanted, cried for.

A mother's love is like the *m* she is made of. It is so abyssal it is almost absurd. A mother's love is ridiculous, pathetic. A mother can't possibly love as much as she does. And the child both wants and does not want the mother's enormous love. But the mother doesn't care; she loves her child, even if the child does not want so much of her love and, worst of all, she loves the child all the more for it. She loves when hating, and hates to love so much. I have seen mothers chewing while they watch their children eat; and cry when their children cry. Mothers are mad. Why do they exist? Why do they love so much? Why do they die? *Por que Deus permite/que as mães vão-se embora?/Mãe não tem limite,/é tempo sem hora: Why does God permit/Mothers to resign/A mother has no limits/ She is hourless time.* For a baby, the mother is the world, an extension of themselves. Psychoanalysts claim that when babies understand their limits, or the difference between themselves and their mothers—the fact that they are babies and that she is another—is the moment the personality, the ego, begins to develop. They also claim that, as adults, narcissists endlessly resent this loss of the mother as extension of the self, which, as a mirror that amplifies only the son's qualities, is the ideal mirror. The narcissist is always searching for his mother; like a baby, he wants this extension of himself to be part of every aspect of his life, throughout his entire life. But he will never have it again; not even if his own mother is present and wants to fulfill this role; she won't be enough. On the contrary, the narcissist will feel anger at her infinite availability. He wants his mother, but not in the shape of a mother, with the voice of a mother. He no longer wants the *mmmmm* that the mother is glad to endlessly repeat.

If the words for mother were *drupra, cratra,* or *rusfala* would we no longer need them as much as we do? Do we need them more than they need us? A mother is autonomous. It is simply enough to be a mother; she can almost do without children. It is already so much to be a mother. But not to be a son. The son always needs a mother; he is nothing on his own. A mother can say: "I am a mother." A son will never say: "I am a son." Being a son is not a status, it's a condition. Not so being a mother. Being a mother is enough for a whole life. Everyone envies the mother because she is a mother. A mother proudly says, "I am a mother," and the father watches her with envy. He will never be a mother. He will always play the supporting role in nature's vertiginous production of continuity, of self-perpetuation. Mothers cannot be understood; the most we know is that they exist.

MONEY

We had no money. Bread was the currency. We could swap a spoon for a piece of bread. When we went to Sweden, we also didn't have money. The Swedes gave us everything: homes, food, jobs, clothing.

She thinks it's good to have money. But she isn't interested, and has never been interested in having much of it—just enough. She is loose with money; the little she has, she gives away. She's doesn't care about saving and doesn't resent that her husband never made much, like her friends' husbands. But he resented it. He wanted to become a millionaire. Not her. She cultivated simple tastes until her husband died, in her seventies. She lived in Bom Retiro, dressed modestly, and always stopped to chat to the people she knew on the street. After his death, she finally moved to Higienópolis and started cultivating more refined tastes. But not much more. She maintains a secret disorder in her fancy house on rua Albuquerque Lins and, even though she goes to the hairdresser once a week (as she did in Bom Retiro), she will always find the cheapest one. She dyes her hair on her own. *Why not? Buying hair dye is so much cheaper than getting your hair dyed at the hairdresser.* She buys cheap clothes (actually, she barely ever buys herself anything at all) and hasn't the remotest idea how to tell a pair of cheap José Paulino jeans from an expensive pair. She simply can't see the difference. When she travels with her daughters, they get annoyed at her frugality. She will always order two dishes, at the most, for three or four people. She makes sure to siphon the water from one bottle into another so that there isn't too much leftover.

She even keeps airplane napkins. But it isn't about saving money; it's about saving. Everything in her fridge is in the smallest portions. She really can't stand it when food goes to waste. It's one of the few things that truly irritate her, seeing things thrown away. And, at the same time, she doesn't understand or know how to recycle plastic, glass, or paper. The anger she feels about waste is much more atavistic than it is ideological.

Father was the complete opposite, maybe even for no other reason than to be contrary, which was one of his favorite activities. He enjoyed spending and wasting. He said it was always important to buy the most expensive things because, here, in Brazil, the most expensive things were always best. He went to expensive restaurants, did not double-check the bill, and tipped generously. He gave his daughters money when they asked for it, without blinking. This must also be an effect of the war. Both frugality and waste are understandable consequences of the war.

Money is, to Jews, a place of residence, perhaps just as much as books. For a diasporic people, doubly exiled after the war, money is more than just a currency of resistance, of survival, it's a place, a map, a home. In Israel, everything is different. Money matters much less there than it does in exile. In Israel, their map is at least nominally guaranteed. However, for the Jewish survivors who left for other countries, money has become a primary topic of conversation, a way of demonstrating a person's capacity to overcome, to resist. Because Jewish survivors had no profession, had not been educated in Brazil—or in the other countries they had emigrated to—did not know how to speak the language, nor knew the customs, they, like many immigrant groups, adopted the language of money. This was their greatest chance of assimilating, and of recovering their lost sense of humanity. Money was—and might even still be—their memory. And perhaps it is also their revenge. The ingrained prejudice that Jews are rich comes from a lack of understanding of a person's need to adopt the language of money, of commerce. Jews, Armenians, Arabs, Japanese—they are all not necessarily rich, they are competent survivors who knew how to find a language that could replace the non-language of suffering from which they came.

When it came to money, her husband fluctuated between two views which, in a way, complemented each other. He wanted to either be a millionaire and own a metallurgy workshop (since he worked in one in Yugoslavia), or he wanted to be a fisherman, who did not need money to survive. Aristocrat or quasi-hippie. In the end, they are very similar. A millionaire also doesn't have to worry about how much money he has, about the practical and bureaucratic details that survival entails. Only millionaires can have the luxury of disdaining the material side of life. The middle class is completely dependent on it, and this morally belittles them. Mother never aspired to these extremes of refinement. She never wanted to be a millionaire or much less, a fisherman. All she wants is her apartment, a full fridge, and well-educated daughters.

When there isn't a regular currency, whether paper, coin, gold, or another precious object, men will immediately make up new forms of commerce. In Auschwitz, bread was money. Half a loaf for a piece of information, a translation, or a cigarette. The Nazis' aims were not financial, but absolutely ideological, and this made them even more exactingly dangerous. Yet, in the Nazis' day-to-day business, what the soldiers instituted in the camps, under the control of the commandants, was of a more commercial nature. Commerce, a form of institutional exchange in which one person possesses more than the other and is able, because of this, to attribute value to a merchandise or good, seems to be an elemental necessity for man. As is the establishment of the notion itself of a hierarchy. Where there is a hierarchy there are more, or less, possessions and where there are possessions, there is commerce. How can we grasp the idea of commerce between people who each possess nothing? How can we come to understand that, when one person possesses no more than a piece of bread, and the other does not possess even that, an economy can still be created? But it was precisely those who knew how to exercise commerce who were able to resist, and to survive.

Dinheiro, money in Portuguese, comes from *dezena*, dozen, just like *dracma*. In English, the word *money* comes from *moeda*, the Portuguese word for coin. *Monetário*, monetary, also has the same root. *Argent* comes from the French word for silver, like *plata*, in Spanish, and the slang, *prata*, in Portuguese. *Geld* comes from *gold* which, like all things in German, is much more concrete. Everything is money. Money is anything: an object, junk, a vegetable, dough, metal, packages, dope. Anything can be made into money and so, in fact, money is no longer anything at all. A recent credit card ad in Brazil made a point of ridiculing people who paid in cash. The thing itself and its abstraction have become one and the same, since they were always the same to begin with. Money is very different from commerce. Commerce is an exchange of real things. Not money. Money is beyond commerce; we don't need commerce for there to be money. Actually, the less commerce, the more money there is.

Jewish survivors, like all survivors, do not know what money is without commerce. They don't know what money is without the gold-thing, the silver-thing, the dozen-thing, the bread-thing. They are peasants, even while they're bourgeois. According to Primo Levi and many other authors, intellectuals were the ones who suffered the most in the camps where, because of the conditions they lived in, everything was turned into commerce. In sub-human conditions, questioning the meaning of things necessarily leads to the loss of physical resistance, and those who resisted commerce had difficulty surviving.

The Jews who arrived in Brazil in the 1950s had the right to a survivor's assistance fund sponsored by the German government. She, her husband, and her mother-in-law requested and received this assistance. Even today, after the deaths of both her husband and her mother-in-law, she still receives a monthly stipend. It's small, but it's something. Her daughter always asked herself if it was right to accept this money. Wasn't it simply a way for the Germans to evade a guilt that could not be repaid? On the other hand, isn't it also a nominally acceptable way of paying for what they did? Should Jewish survivors be asking for more? Or should they refuse, categorically? But can anything be gained from refusing? If this is done in order to expropriate the guilty, they should at least accept some help.

Everything that relates to war, and especially this war, is cause for dilemma, even sixty years later. And even having a dilemma is a dilemma; the children of survivors are much more accustomed to moral conflicts than even the survivors themselves. José Miguel Wisnik, a professor of Brazilian Literature and a composer, said the following, which sums up the difference between survivors and their children: do not dramatize a tragedy. Those who have experienced this dry tragedy, this close cut, do not feel moral dramas. Theirs is a different morality. Those who haven't experienced it, who have only heard tell the story, who are both close and far, can only dramatize it. Those who envy tragedy dramatize it.

STONE 2

Tragedy-as-stone. Drama-as-stone.

TRAGEDY–AS–STONE

Founded by Xeno of Citium, Stoicism affirms that the universe is material and exists under the command of a divine logos, *a concept borrowed from Heraclitus. The soul identifies with this divine principle, as part of a whole to which it belongs. This* logos *(or universal reason) ordains everything: everything arises from it and in accordance with it; and it is thanks to it that the world is a* kosmos *(which in Greek means "harmony").*

Stoicism posits life in accordance with a rational law of nature, and counsels indifference (apathea) *toward everything that is external to one's being. The wise man obeys this natural law by recognizing that he is no more than a player in the grand order and purpose of the universe, and that he must stay serene through the tragic as well as the good.[1]*

The entire universe is material. To carry a stone above one's head in a concentration camp in 1944 is to be part of the body of the universe. It is to be the hand, finger, liver, and spleen of the universe. It is to be the star, the tree trunk, the stone itself, to meld with the corporeality of the stone. It is to become part of another planet, where others also carry stones, or where bacteria wander wildly through a swamp, or perhaps where there is nothing at all, and to carry a stone is to carry nothing.

The universe is material and exists under the command of a divine

---

1   Taken from the *Stanford Encyclopedia of Philosophy.*

logos, *a concept borrowed from Heraclitus.* According to Heraclitus, *logos* is the underlying reason, the cosmic order that governs everything that takes place in the material universe. It is, in other words, an idea similar to that of God—a God who commands and sets down rules and who, behind all these rules and regulations is also incomprehensibly good. This hand, this spleen of the universe, which carries the stone, this star from another galaxy, is also part of a cosmic order and is governed by an order—order, ordinance, organization, regulations, bureaucracy, convention, system, doctrine, ideology, legislation, classification, hierarchy, structure, schematization, plan, process, method, procedure, sequence—which would like, in some secret unknowable way, for that stone, in that instant and in that place, to be carried by that person—in this case, Mother. Zeno of Citium and, before him, Heraclitus, created a system of the notion that, behind that stone she carried, there was a *logos*—which later become *word, reason*—which wanted, determined, and knew that she would carry that stone. The act of submitting to carrying the stone is to be part of the cosmic order, to carry out the harmonious will of the governing reason. To refuse to carry it would be disobey this will, superior to that of the individual Nazi official, who is a mere instrument of the cosmic will. And what if a person were to disobey? What if one would rather die than carry the stone? Wouldn't this also be part of the universal *logos*'s will?

The soul identifies with this divine principle, as of a whole to which it belongs. This logos *(or universal reason) ordains everything: everything arises from it and in accordance with it; and it is thanks to it that the world is a* kosmos *(which in Greek means "harmony").*

What is a person's soul at the exact moment she carries a stone above her head? Being part of the body, the soul carries the stone with the body. Actually, it is the soul, not the body, that carries it, because in this instant soul and body are one and the same. If the soul cannot bear what the body must do, they separate, becoming two, breaking the universe's cosmic unity. The finger separates from the hand; the soul, separate and disobedient, displeases the universal *logos* and, because of this rupture, minimal as it may be, there is an earthquake, a storm, a sudden change in season. It is hotter in winter and colder in summer.

The *logos* (or universal reason) ordains everything: everything arises from it and in accordance with it; it is thanks to the *logos* that the world is a *kosmos*. The *logos* ordains, it organizes, it commands. To organize is to command. It is to set the napkins and the plates, with the cutlery on the correct side, the main dish and the salad; everything set just right for the guests. The person who organizes the table, commands the table—a universal principle of harmony—and sits at the head of the table. The organizer is the commander. To order: to command, to demand obedience. What is the intimate distinction between the cosmic order—spring, summer, fall, winter, day, night, flowers, leaves, fruit, birth, life and death—and an officer's order: *do it now!? Schnell!?* Is *logos* an officer who stands at the top (or bottom) of the universe giving orders? *Pick up the stone! Carry it! Live! Die!*

Everything arises from it and in accordance with it. From it: the universal source of everything. *In accordance with it:* in its image and likeness. Everyone carries the image and likeness of the universal *logos*. What does it look like? It must be protean, in the form of all that acts and exists. It is the image and likeness of everything which, arising from it, takes place. What is the difference between image and likeness? Some exegetes must have spent decades discussing, challenging, and analyzing it. The image of the *logos*. Image is an indirect thing. And what takes place is simply a likeness of the image. First world, third world, barely sentient world, and so far from the intelligible world, where the *logos* surely does not carry stones, being as it is part of the whole. The person who carries a stone here, in the sentient world, in the world of images and likenesses, is no more than a poor imitation of the pure *logos,* which does not carry stones.

Stoicism posits life in accordance with a rational law of nature and counsels indifference (apathea) *toward everything that is external to one's being.*

Carrying a stone is external to oneself. One stone, picked out of hundreds of thousands of stones all piled in a corner of the camp. To grab the stone, and take the stone to a specific point, where the ground is covered in gravel, and hold it there throughout the whole day. The stone is not a sentient being; one can therefore be simply apathetic, and indifferent, toward it. Stoicism posits living *in accordance with* the rational law of nature. Again, *in accordance with*. It is what it is, if it must be so. Whatever happens, happens. Fate is what happens. The past is what has passed. In accepting the tragic, therefore, there is no submission, but simply a kind of foreknowledge or even a retrospective knowledge. A prophecy of the real. What is happening is what is happening. There is no quitters' apathy, only the wisdom of the connoisseur. A kind of superiority. The tragic accepts, because it could have been no different. If it had been different, the cosmic unity would have been broken.

The wise man obeys the natural law by recognizing that he is no more than a player in the grand order and purpose of the universe, and that he must stay serene through the tragic as well as the good.

Order and purpose of the universe. Besides order, the universal *logos* also has a purpose and it is not man's responsibility to know or to question it. Everything has happened on purpose and with a purpose. Children will often say, when they have been found out, that they did not do it on purpose, that is was *by accident.* In the universe, though, nothing is excused. Carelessness, clumsiness, forgetting, accidents—what purpose do these serve? The universe has a finality; and the person who carries the stone can see herself as a player in the grand order and purpose of the universe. Why did she carry the stone? We don't know, nor will we ever know. But, according to Stoicism, there must have been a purpose.

The wise man must remain serene in the face of the tragic and the good. Serenity: silence. Serene: cloudless. The wise man must remain silent and cloudless, like a sky in which we see no signs of rain. Neither the body nor the soul, which in the wise man are one and the same, may show signs of alteration in their serenity. Healthy mind in a healthy body. To carry the stone serenely, with a silent soul. *Mom, what did you think of while you were carrying that stone? Nothing, love, nothing. I couldn't think. I cried, but I couldn't wipe away my tears.*

DRAMA-AS-STONE

Rubric: theater
bourgeois drama

Form of tragedy recognized at the end of the 18th century by Denis Diderot (1713-1784) with the replacement of Greco-Roman characters by bourgeois citizens in settings that reflected the conditions of their social status.

Rubric: theater
Lachrymose drama

The word drama has its origins in Ancient Greek, meaning "to act."

Drama is a theatrical genre that aims to create the highest possible tension in the spectator; the audience finds itself "captured" by what takes place on stage as they attempt to guess what comes next, while also idealizing each character's end.

Drama-as-stone is the unbearable, the un-serene, a cloudy sky, the unwise. Drama-as-stone are questions like: but why did you surrender? Why didn't you prefer to die? Did no one walk by while you were holding the stone? Did no one help? Where did the stone come from? How long did you hold the stone? Why did he choose this punishment? Did your cousins not apologize? Did they not regret it forever? How could you forgive them? Drama-as-stone is the guilt, the fear, the incomprehension; it is holding the stone in her place, it is feeling the spiritual, exaggerated, false pain that she thinks her mother felt.

Tragedy is a clean cut; Drama is a slow sharpening. Tragedy does; Drama undoes and redoes. Tragedy knows; Drama seeks to know. Tragedy does not think; Drama interprets. Tragedy is; Drama imitates.

The drama of the dramatic is that it has not experienced tragedy. It is a moment, a derivative, a reverse, a shadow, a however. The dramatic writes the tragic because the tragic isn't written, it is the mirror of things that happen; no, it is the thing as it happens. The dramatic of the dramatic is that it writes; it is the thereafter. What is it like to be thereafter? The thereafter chokes, it does not understand, it wants nothing more than to understand, and always more than the tragic was ever capable of. The dramatic goes to Auschwitz in 2009 and does not know what to do, where to begin, what to feel, what to search for. The dramatic does not know if its trip is objective, informative, documentary, poetic, nostalgic, dumb, useless, touristic, individual, collective, or familiar; if it is false, true, recuperative, transformative, alive, dead, capricious, careful, dreamy, neutral, ridiculous, absolving, egoistic, narcissistic, or interesting; if there is no exit, if it is educational; if its purpose is to remember or to forget; if it is tiring, strong, fragile, enriching, impoverishing, verifiable, or innocent. The dramatic knows nothing. It goes to Auschwitz in the winter because it wants to feel at least a margin of the cold the tragic felt, but it bundles up. It would be too absurd to dress down. It would be a ridiculous flight of fancy to want to feel what the prisoners felt. Like one of those trips millionaires take, paying a fortune to be beggars for a day. Or is it? Is it absurd to want to experience the suffering a person very close to you has felt, to come to know the smallest amount of their pain?

Is it absurd to want the knowledge of this pain and, inevitably, to live behind this knowledge? The dramatic does not have a choice. It is simply dramatic, which is why it is laughable, and every attempt it makes is an imitation—legitimate, but absurd.

Leave tragedy be! Let it be what it is: a stone. *I can't,* says the dramatic. And it really can't. The only ones who can leave it be are the tragic or the comic.

But drama also has its upside. The drama-as-stone will only be any good if it also admits its own absurdity, if it does not let itself be fooled by pain and try to be what it is not—tragic.

LOVE

I used to have a boyfriend and, in the camp, when the boys were marching, I kept looking for him. I thought about him a lot. Before they took us, we fought, and I never saw him again. He had flirted with another girl to provoke me. After the war, he wrote to me asking that we get back together again, that I should go to Israel, but I didn't want to.

She kept looking for her boyfriend in the camp. Father, the man she would later marry, had been in a labor camp, not an extermination camp, like she had. In the fabular memory of the daughter who is telling this story and trying to remember how her father used to tell it himself, the camp was in Austria, and it was small, with no more than nine hundred prisoners. She does not recall the name of the camp, which he repeated often and yet no one can seem to remember. Father would say that it had almost been good there. He slept in a stable, which was not too cold, woke up early in the morning to clean the cow manure and worked little throughout the rest of the day. The way the daughter remembers it, he even had a girlfriend.

Dating in concentration camps. There are very few, or perhaps even no stories at all, about people who dated in those conditions. But there are many accounts of distraction, and even of pleasure. Primo Levi and Ruth Klüger both wrote that when they recited poems, or read aloud excerpts of novels, they'd forget they were in the camp, and the people who were listening to them read would experience true moments of joy. And it's clear that people formed habits in the camps, as they do in other places in the world, as awful as they may be, habits which contain and lead to distraction. Distraction is essential to survival; those who concentrate constantly will likely not survive. But it's also necessary for the person to grow accustomed to horror in order to be able to overcome it; to create routines, rituals, symbols. And distraction: to talk about food, to remember poems, holidays, to pray, talk, tell stories. To distract oneself is to go off the beaten track. In order to survive, we have to be on track yet also able to occasionally escape; a verse is also a version, poetry is a version that is off track. Versions, lies, simulations, stories, are all necessary to survival. In order to survive—to survive survival itself—in order to continue, to remember, to forget, to remember.

But loving: flirting, dating, hugging, kissing, having sex, jealousy, games, strategies, gazes, laughs. Yes?

Mother is so beautiful. To this day, she has the loveliest legs, few wrinkles, and a well-defined body. One of Mother's friends, whom her daughter met in Israel, says she once asked Father: *How could Lili possibly want to marry you? You're so ugly!* But, since life is in the hands of fate, as Mother says, they married. She did not marry the man she loved, but another, yet in her view everything happened as it should, and she is grateful for it.

After they met in what was once Yugoslavia, Father had to return to Hungary with his mother. She thought they would never see each other again and, because he had declared his love for her, she gave him her diary, which she'd started to write in Malmö, Sweden. It was a considerate souvenir, something to remember her by. In the last few pages of this diary, which today is in the Yad Vashem museum in Jerusalem, he wrote her love letters, in which he claimed he could not live without her, that she was so lovely, he would marry no other.

When she handed over her diary to the museum, the Yugoslav employees there read it to the end and were curious to know if the two had stayed together. When she went back to the museum and told them that, yes, they had, the women celebrated. Theirs was a love story with a happy ending, they said. And she would say this, too, but not with the same enthusiasm, because her happy ending is not one that ends in love. She is happy because she came to Brazil, had three daughters, and built a home, because her husband was honest and hard-working, her daughters studied, and they were able to buy a house, and this is what was meant to be. But she never again felt the kind of love she had felt for her first boyfriend.

Father had a completely different idea of love. He was enthusiastic, passionate, and fiery. He had always been in love with her and had wanted to live his love fully, even if he didn't know what that might mean. An imaginary love. She accepted his real love, which was translated into gestures, habits, commitment, and family. Their daughter asks herself if her father idealized love so much because he hadn't suffered as her mother had. Does greater suffering make people more accepting of difficulties? It both does and doesn't. Suffering to an extent that is absurd, unspeakable, and muted is a bodily assault, and the body senses and retains those fears that harm it. It does not want to suffer any longer. And so it avoids everything that is either acutely good or bad. A body that has suffered wants only the neutral, and love is neutral. But, on the other hand, once the suffering has passed, life also wants to come to life again, and with it the pain, because then life will forget its suffering. Life is both intelligent and stupid, and intelligence and stupidity have equal force.

One day in 2011, the daughter found a few loose papers in a grammar book from 1961, on which were jotted some grammar lessons her parents had been studying. Conjugations of the verbs *to love* and *to go*, along with the classifications of Portuguese pronouns. In her mother's handwriting: *eu amo, tu amas, ele ama, nós amamos, vós amais, eles amam; I love, you love, he loves, we love, you love, they love*. The daughter teaches Brazilian Literature; she knows how to conjugate every verb in Portuguese. Her mother doesn't. To this day, she doesn't know how to conjugate *love*, nor any other verb in Portuguese. Mother doesn't remember these grammar lessons; her daughter handles these papers as if she were the one learning Portuguese. The daughter thinks to herself how she happened to be writing about love and found a piece of paper on which her mother had learned how to conjugate the verb *love*.

What is her mother's love like? *What makes me happy is when you are happy. What I most want is what you most want. I like the three of you equally. It's impossible to know which one of you I like best. It would be like choosing one of the fingers of my hand.* Mother's love is (became) the love of a mother. Pot-as-love, home-as-love, wall-as-love, time-as-love.

Flaubert spoke of parrot words; words that are repeated again and again and therefore lose all meaning. He said that one mother-parrot-word is *universe. Love* is also a mother-parrot-word.

LOVE 2

They say:

I love as love loves. I know no other reason to love but to love you. What would you have me say, other than I love you, when what I want to say is that I love you? Love is big and fits in this window above the sea. The sea is big and fits in the bed and blankets of loving. Love is big and fits in the brief space of kissing. Love, because there is nothing better for your health than requited love. The measure of love is to love without measure. To love is not to accept everything. Actually: where everything is accepted, I fear there may be love lacking. Man loves…because love is the essence of his soul—because he cannot help loving. The pleasure of love is in loving; we are happier in the passion we feel than in the passion we inspire. Loving others is the only form of individual salvation I know: no one who gives love will be lost and they may even receive love in return. Love sought is good, but given unsought better. God, to man's delight, invented faith and love. The Devil, in envy, made man confuse faith with religion and love with marriage. It is so good to die of love! And to continue living. Love does not consist in gazing at each other, but in looking outward together in the same direction.

If we all love, why do people want to know what love is? Is loving a thing or a practice? People wonder why so few can stand its force, its weight, its burden, its shapelessness. They want to know if their love is just like the love others feel, that their other feels. Love is both cultural and innate; its internal and external force is of such a dimension that men think that if they are able to understand it they will be able to better dominate it. Please, explain what love is. Explain why she can't help looking for her boyfriend in the concentration camp. Is love a consolation? A necessity? A blessing? Is it the meaning of life? *Mom,* she asks on the phone, *what's the meaning of life? I think it's your kids. Isn't it? Isn't it that for you, too? But, what's the meaning of life before you have kids? I think it's getting married.* They laugh and laugh. *To get married and then have kids. But, before we even get to that, I think the meaning of life is to study. Right?* Having children must mean the same as loving one's children. That is what love is to her and that is enough, because fate would have it so. According to her daughter, life doesn't only have one meaning. At least this is what she says, ostentatiously exhibiting her disbelief in destiny. According to her, the fact that life lacks meaning allows it to have infinite meaning; there are different meanings for every day, for every need or desire, or, sometimes, no meaning at all. Only that it happens when it happens. But, when her mother says that the meaning of life is to have children, she feels herself soften. And she agrees.

Love must be the mother-parrot-word. Because it is in everything.

IN AUSCHWITZ

Tour guide: *And now we'll go to the gas chambers.*

The old prisoner's barracks are now blocks, each separated by nationality. There's the Hungarian block, the Romanian block, the Yugoslav block, and the Greek block. The doors to the Hungarian block are like the doors to the bank in *The Trial*. When K walks by those doors he hears the sounds of a beating. Opening the door, he sees a man being beaten. He asks what is happening. The beater responds: *I am a beater, I beat.*

There is a sign in the general exhibition that reads: *The one who doesn't remember history is bound to live through it again.* Mauricio Santayana.

Correspondence between Germans detailing the various amounts of money taken from Jews:

124,940 zlotys

20,415 rubles

15,577 karbovantsi

567 Thou. Kronen

828.1 Belg. francs

5 US dollars

1,858 Rom. lei

Secret messages from the camp's resistance movement to a clandestine organization:

9, 314, 7, 4, 3, 2, 8, 7-180-14, 5, 11, 16, 11-24, 27, 31-7, 27, 31-7, 27, 26-11, 18, 3, 7, 11, 12, 91.

A calculation demonstrating the cost of constructing a crematorium: 19,000 Deutsche Marks.

The cost of the installation of the ventilators in the crematorium.

Zyklon B: the registered trademark of an acid, chlorine- and nitrogen-based pesticide that was used by the Nazis as a poison for mass-murder by suffocation of the prisoners in the gas chambers, and which was activated when it came into contact with the air. The name derives from the German nouns for its main ingredients and the letter B is one of its different concentrations. This compound was chosen because it efficiently facilitated a quick death. The main components of the product were hydrocyanic acid, chlorine, and nitrogen. Hydrocyanic acid is very poisonous to superior animals such as humans. The LD_{50} corresponds to 1mg/kg and is a very volatile liquid, with a boiling point at 25.6°C. It has a half-life of 20 to 60 min. It smells strongly of bitter plums. HCN is used through its absorption in inert substances —in the case of Zyklon B, in solids, and of Zyklon A, in liquids.

It is principally absorbed through inhalation. The way in which gas reacts in the organism in cases of acute intoxication, are mydriasis, convulsion, muscular rigidity, and respiratory paralysis.

Hair: locks, loose braids, grayish tufts. 1,950 kg of hair. Hair was sold to German industrial businesses as a raw material for 50 pfennigs a kilogram.

Names: Tadeusz Jude, Roman Nadolski, Roman Yopala, Karl Kassler, Lao Rajner, Pola Fogilman, Sima Szfranska, Raquel Zucker, Michela Rayktop, Sara Pachet, Lotte Neuman, Rita Mano.

A telegraph recounting the death of rabbi Szmuel Kornitzer of Krakow.

Combs, shaving brushes, prostheses, glasses, buckets, pans, kettles, chamber pots, bowls, dishes, cookers, burners, plates, graters, thermos bottles, sieves, rolling pins, baby bottles, spoons, scales, measurers.

Two displays full of shoes.

Suitcases: Zlenka Fantl; Manski Alois, Wien, Podenstrass, 22; Margarete Glase, 14/08/1897; Marie Kafka, Prag, XII, 833; Herman Pasternak; Benjamin Lazarus; Raphaela Sata Tansik, II Blumaeurgrass.

Baby clothes.

Headless dolls.

Red triangle: political prisoners.

Green triangle: criminals.

Black triangle with Z or brown triangle: Roma.

Black triangle: asocial prisoners.

Yellow SU letters: Russian POWs.

Pink triangle: homosexuals.

Purple triangle: Jehovah's witnesses.

Striped uniforms.

Each block held 700 to 1,000 prisoners.

In the bathroom, there is a painting of two kittens licking themselves, a reminder of good hygiene. A child washing another with a pot of water.

ANGER 2

We were angry at our kapo. *She was a prisoner, too, but after five years of forced labor, no longer had a heart. They would take the meat from our soup. They were Jews, like us, but they were worse than the Germans. Suffering hardens people.*

The daughter always asks herself what she would have done if she had been there; and her answer is always that it's impossible to know. Would she rather have died? Would she have had the disposition to help someone? Would she have been cruel? Her mother seems to never have been cruel. On the contrary, she tells of how she always helped others, whenever she could, since she herself had been incredibly lucky to be chosen to work in the kitchen. She talks about how she once took stolen quinine to a boy who had cholera, and handed it to him through the electric fence. Do you have to be lucky not to be cruel? The soldiers would hold competitions to see who could kill the most Jews with a single bullet; some would practice target shooting, from a distance. The *kapo* stole the meat from the prisoners' soups.

As a child, the daughter once frightened herself when she realized she felt pleasure in poking and hurting a little bird inside its cage. The pleasure of helping another for no reason, or even in exchange for something, may be the civilized evolution of a much simpler pleasure—watching someone suffer. This initial, vital impulse is sadistic. Once the motivation for man's humanity is taken from him, all that is left is a perverse inclination, which can become creativity and transformation, or simply humiliation and suffering.

Where there is suffering, it seems imperative that everyone suffer and that the other suffer more than everyone else. A little power in a place of great suffering is still a lot of power. People fight tenaciously so that they can have even the slightest amount of power, as mediocre as it might be; as if this power represented a rare force and attributed to the little person who holds this power the right to offhandedly and gratuitously arbitrate over the prisoner's life and microrights. *Oh, so you have the right to one hundred grams of bread? I guess I'll give you eighty. Why? Just so I can feel that I am exerting power over you.*

There are many possible ways to exert power and even to suffer. People suffer stoically, humiliatingly, heroically, morally, spiritually, physically, collectively, individually. How can we go about measuring, and judging suffering under these conditions? How can we judge the sufferer's actions? Relatedly, power also suffers variations in degree, content, and abuse. What to do with an extra loaf of bread? Distribute it, barter it, eat it, keep it, sell it? What do each of these frames of mind say about each person's true self? In states of absolute privation, does that thing we call personality even exist? The daughter loves to imagine she would have been stoic and capable in those conditions, a member of the concentration camp's underground resistance movement. How absurd! Strength and courage are not only on the side of defiance, and retrospective self-idealization is an illness that requires urgent care.

To live one's day-to-day in a free city, in a free country as if there were always some danger to be fought off, and to participate in a movement that rebels against the system even when there is no real oppression to fight. A sly, inexplicit rebellion that is practiced daily, on the smallest of things. To always say no; to live on a diet of "no." To say yes, to be naïve, silly, and foolish, as a way of rebelling against the ruling intelligentsia. To mirror herself in her mother's innocence. Yes as no. To denounce herself, break herself in the name of others, uselessly, because this is what her mother did. If she could it, so can her daughter. A pathology of dumb courage. An affirmation of her individuality, the poetry of a sole identity, which is actually no more than a compulsive mirroring. Atoning for her own guilt; revenging her mother. The kind of courage a person is capable of. To the daughter, even fear is courage.

The daughter is not afraid. Her way of being is active. She gets angry in advance, acts first and fixes things later. She can't stand inertia, patience, silence, or conjecture. The future is under constant construction, and does not exist beforehand. Things have no meaning. Everything depends on action, which gradually creates our senses of geography, ethics, and time. Take it and go! She does not like to give time to time. She hates order, that exacting, tantalizing, tautological, and arbitrary animal. She hates power, order's cadaverous brother, and fear, which is death grafted onto life.

ANGER 3

Perversity and perversion

Perversity: of a bad nature or character; depravity; corruption.
Perversion: the alteration of a thing from its natural state; a turn
in behavior.

Perverse and perverted. The perverse, according to the dictionary,
are intrinsically, naturally bad. The perverted, however, is one who
has suffered an alteration, who has gone off-track, or changed
direction. The perverted, therefore, are not necessarily perverse.
The perverse are naturally perverted, which means they are not
necessarily perverted, as they have not changed direction, but were
instead born that way. But, if they were already born that way and if
that is their nature, or their character, why the root *verse*? What has
turned, changed? Did they turn from goodness, from their innately
human character? Is it possible to become perverse, or are those
who become perverse actually simply perverted and therefore
deserving of more consideration, since their perversion might be
mitigated by the difficult circumstances that created it? But if the
perverse are born this way, if this is their character, how can we condemn them? How can we condemn a person for their character?

What's the difference between the cruel, the perverse, the sadistic, the bad, and the wicked?

The cruel take pleasure in blood and spill blood. The cruel are
implacable.

The perverse are simply that, perverse.

A sadist is one who takes sexual pleasure in the humiliation or physical suffering of others.

The wicked have bad fortune, bad luck.

The bad is of poor quality; it is erroneous, misshapen, deformed.

The wicked are wretched. They do not exercise meanness, but wickedness. They have suffered the bitterness of fate and therefore react childishly by committing robberies, minor transgressions, and pranks. The wicked are bootlickers, amateur evildoers who will never be promoted; on the grand scale of Great Evil, they are laughable.

Sadists are aesthetes of the suffering of others; their ends are erotic and voyeuristic. The sadist is a creator, who likes beauty and refined suffering, who would like the sufferer to suffer, but not to the point where it turns ugly. The sadist isn't cruel and will often have received some kind of consent from the sufferer, also known as a masochist, the sadist's counterpart. One cannot exist without the other.

The cruel are cooked medium rare. As if they had not experienced civilization or culture; as if they had distanced and isolated themselves in some remote place far from ethics' often loose threads. They are implacable. They do not understand fear, forgiveness, or compassion, and when they want to do something, they do it. An act is more important than its merit, its content. They do not act out of some sort of internal, individual evil, but because it must be done. Action is what is most important. They do not act in the name of evil, but in the name of the action itself.

Evil is pure as is Good. Evil is the direct, unmediated product of evil itself, of the Devil, and of the Platonic idea of evil. Does evil exist? Are the purely evil, the truly evil, also so with their wives, their kids? They must be; if they are evil, they must be so always; otherwise, they are not evil. The evil cannot have been victims of a pathology, or have experienced difficulties during their childhood that would have turned them evil. They must be like those evil characters in fairy tales who appear out of nowhere and threaten and decimate Good. Evil is feared by Good.

But this is not the case with the perverse. The perverse were not necessarily born evil. They have walked the paths of culture; they have experienced it. They have known wellness and good, and are able to act accordingly with their families and with a chosen few. They selectively exercise evil. And selection is the key word. It was the War's word. The perverse select; they arbitrate over the criteria of how to measuredly administrate evil. They take delight in the sophisticated suffering of the chosen, and take pleasure in sharing it with their perverse colleagues. The perverse have colleagues. The evil do not; nor do the cruel. The cruel and the evil are solitary; they do not want nor know how to share. The perverse need exposure; they need to exhibit their victories. They have ideological justifications for their acts of humiliation, both for themselves, and for others, who will eventually support them, and for those who attempt to understand them, they have antecedents that might explain their perversion. What a deceptive word, perversion. As if the justification for the exercise of evil were intrinsic to the word itself. In the end, the perverted have perverted only themselves, which has a certain passivity to it, as if to pervert oneself were synonymous to letting oneself be perverted. As if men were victims of family, circumstance, and society. The perverse are evil in themselves, but more than those who are evil. The devil is evil and the devil does not act on earth, but in hell, and on those with whom we have no relation.

Perversity is the worst of evils.

FEAR

I wasn't afraid of dying. I wasn't afraid at all, but I did everything I could to stay alive.

She says, *I wasn't afraid at all,* as if she'd felt the need to feel afraid, as if she'd made the effort to feel fear, but hadn't been able to. Perhaps animalization lessens fear to the point of suppressing it. The animalized man wants to eat; he wants more than he fears. He fears not eating, buts does not fear dying because he is already dead. But the conditions she was in were not as inhumane as those of others—she worked in the kitchen. She wasn't afraid because she had already lost almost everything. In a situation such as hers, maybe there was simply nothing left to fear. When she says she was not afraid, is it true? She says, *I wasn't afraid at all,* and so this must be the case. Sometimes fear can feel like a presence; its absence leaves a person feeling lonelier than they are by nature. Fear gives man a feeling for life, a feeling of dependence and of privation, which in a way, fulfills him. But the camp suppresses even this.

Even today, she fears nothing. She fears only for her children and grandchildren to fall ill. But she does not fear old age, illness, degeneracy, and she does not fear death. She lives each day as if it were her only day, her last day, and also as if it were just another day. At eighty-five, she is very healthy. When someone dies, especially someone she is close to, she does not, to her daughters' astonishment, feel scared, nor does she feel very sad. She accepts it. Her daughters become indignant, as if her attitude indicated a certain negligence on her part toward the people she supposedly loved.

Even when her brother, who lived in the United States, died, all she said when she called her daughter was *My brother died. Call around, find his number, and send my condolences to Lilika*. She didn't know the number. Her daughter had to spend hours looking for it before she finally found it. Then she called her mother to say she had found the number, and asked if she wanted some company that night. *No, I don't need a thing. And, no, I don't want to go there. He didn't come here when Daddy died, why would I go there now? He's dead, I don't have to go to the funeral*. All this might sound like a sort of pragmatism that conceals a fear of death, or like a way of evading fear. But it isn't. It's both a great fondness for life itself and for her own life; it's the acceptance that life is simple and inevitable. It is forgetting in action. When she hears about the death of someone close to her, she sets this process of forgetting into gear. One must forget, and then forget again. Forgetting is the absence of fear. Those who remember, fear. It is memory that is the present's source of pain. The present, charged with the memory of past pains, awakens fear, which is a physical defense against the recurrence of this pain. Fear is past and future. Those who live only in the present, as she does, do not fear, or at least fear less.

When her daughters or grandchildren travel, she only ever asks about the trip itself. She isn't interested in how they are, or what they're doing, but she needs to know whether they've arrived, departed, or if they've gone off to some distant place. It's almost as if what worried her was the act of displacement, not the visit itself. Danger exists only in their displacement. Compared to the lukewarm temperature at which she has lived her life, to her, this movement burns like a fever or hypothermia. Nevertheless, she enjoys traveling herself and, unafraid of death, adapts easily to transitioning from one place to another.

She also isn't afraid of losing anything. She doesn't fear being mugged, or misplacing any of her possessions or objects. She has given herself to life with an open heart and has let it freely run its course. She faced and continues to face the world without the need to fight, or to defend herself. Because she is here, and this is the lot she was given.

Her daughters aren't afraid of much, either: not of growing old, or ugly, nor of traveling, or not having money, not of losses, violence, travel, nor of social situations, of gossip, or slander. The three of them are strong. You might even say they're warriors, even though it is far too ridiculous a word to use to characterize living since at the end of the day, living is not, and should not be, like waging a war. But they're brave. And in that sense, you can also say they're victors. At least when it comes to the decisions they make or the adventures they set out on. They don't wait, they act. And then they fix—or sometimes not—the problems they'd encountered in their undertaking. But they won't ever not act because they fear something might not work out.

Maybe the only thing she really fears is having to depend on someone in order to live. Fear of indignity. She doesn't want to be an inconvenience. She's said many times that if she were to fall ill, she would like to be sent to a nursing home, or a retirement home. And she doesn't fear this prospect, as many of the elderly do. Her daughter thinks she might even adapt well to a retirement home, if need be. She would play cards, which she does better than anyone, and chat with her friends. She would go to bed and wake up and live one more day.

Fear is the worst enemy of life, she'd say.

SPOKESPERSON

The spokesperson is the keeper of speech. She hears the speech not spoken, takes it, and keeps it in her pocket, carrying it as if it were no more than a wallet, or a set of keys. Then, she, the spokesperson, imparts to others those things that she has found in that kept speech. As if she were simply removing from her wallet documents, abandoned or forgotten papers, coins, photographs, bills, expired credit cards, an old prayer, two matches, a toothpick, two bank statements, a dentist's bill, or a shopping list. But she also removes from her wallet things that are not even there, because she is the keeper of speeches that have not been spoken, and might not even know how to be spoken if they had to.

The spokesperson is the worst kind of thief. The owner of the speech lets her steal it, but she steals more than what the owner has allowed, leaving the owner mute. She is speechless. The speech owner is now obligated to hear what the spokesperson says and to accept that this is what she would also say. Or worse, what she would not even be capable of saying. The spokesperson steals the speech owner's speech and surpasses it, playing it like a fiddle.

Is the spokesperson envious?

The spokesperson carries with her the most precious thing a person can have. Why does the speech owner let the spokesperson carry her words? Why does she not speak herself? The speech owner does not speak because: she cannot, she does not have the ability or time to, she does not remember, she cannot control it, she has not mastered it, or she cannot articulate it. So she gives another the permission to articulate her thoughts and opinions.

Go on, keep them. But what are they, speech owner? I don't know. But I trust you. Make it up.

When the speech owner has forgotten her words, or has not even been able to formulate them, and a person comes to her and asks to carry her speech, she lets them. *Remember those things I've forgotten. Don't tell me about them. I don't want to remember. You're doing this for you, not for me. I am giving you my speech and my memories because I don't care about them—you do. So get on with it. Keep them, dig in.*

MEMORY

"Remember, forget – what's the difference to me?"
(Bill Rose in *The Bellarosa Connection* by Saul Bellow)

Remembering and forgetting are very similar. They are selective mnemonic processes, which relate to the past—recent or distant—and are charged with both reality and invention. If we remember not only what has happened, but also what we would like to have happened, why can we not also say that we have forgotten things that have not happened, or that we would have liked not to happen?

Some fear remembering and so they turn the present into a burden, into a mass made up of the past. Others can't bear to remember; to them, the present can also be a mass made up of forgetting. *Look at all I've forgotten!* they say. What is forgotten is not a hollow mass, the opposite of the dense mass of remembering. What is forgotten can be a fully solid mass, filled with images and words that do not speak. You ask them and they stay silent, refusing to open their eyes or to be seen. The forgotten past is a Medusa: when she looks into the eyes of those who call to her persistently, she paralyzes the gazes of the ones who see and who will from then on remain wide-eyed and open-mouthed, forever. What has been forgotten cannot be remembered with impunity. To dig out the memory of forgetting is to stick your hands into mountains and labyrinths and mirrors and pyramids of garbage, dirt, monsters, and distorted images, to the point where a scene of a mother cooking can easily be linked to a scene of torture.

Esquecer—"to forget" in Portuguese—is to fall outside: *ex cadere*. To slip, to stoop, to fall. The forgetter drops out. Or more accurately, it is the forgetter's recollections that fall out of his memory. The forgetter slips out of time. He stands at the edge of the current, and observes time from another place—a place of privilege, relegated by those who remember. But those who remember will not allow the forgetter to forget too much. They quarrel with him: *Remember! Come on, now, remember. How come you don't know?* There is something obsessive, something compulsive about those who remember; they will not settle. They win at memory games, they remember lists, put together spreadsheets, they advise, they warn, and worst of all, they repeat the phrase, *Don't say I didn't tell you so.* They can even remember the future and will inform the forgetter that he will inevitably forget everything he must remember. The forgetter really does forget. He is indebted to those who remember. Then he asks for forgiveness. And those who remember may or may not give it. Memory is a tyrant and the memory of those who remember is the worst of them all.

If to forget is to fall outside, then this means there is an inside. Inside is time, which runs normally: days, months, years. But what's outside? What exists outside memory? Do dreams live inside or outside memory? It is like being outside language. But what is there outside language? There must still be sensations, intuitions, sounds, and shapes, but nothing that can be spoken. As soon as something is spoken, it disappears, and quickly becomes the "inside." There, now it's a word. It is inside. Those on the inside say to those on the outside, *Come, come on in. You'll catch a cold out there. Careful. Stay inside where you'll be safer.*

Some of those who are outside end up agreeing and making their way inside, so that they may be under the protection and care of the hours and minutes of the clocks. Others don't. They're prone to relapsing, either due to resistance or negligence. They stay there, on the outside, living outside time. Sometimes they peek through the cracks at the inside spaces, but only to see what's happening. Those who are inside grow scared. *Look, a shadow! Quick, let's go see what it's about.* And then those things they have forgotten flee, in fear or laughter.

In English, *to forget* comes from the German word, *vergessen.* Both in German and in English, *forget* and *forgive* have the same roots, and are almost the same. *Vergessen* and *vergeben.* To forgive and forget. When God forgives a sin, it is forgotten. The Jewish God remembers everything. The Jews are the memory of God and God is their memory. But it is not so with Christianity. A Christian God forgets. Forgives and forgets. Forgiving must therefore also mean "for giving." God gives, concedes forgiveness and then forgets the sin. Does this mean that when humans forget things, they have forgiven themselves, or have they forgiven the person who has inflicted pain on them? Is forgetting oneself forgiving? For humans, forgetting may be to never forgive. We forget because we cannot forgive.

What does forgiveness mean to mankind? Primo Levi never forgave. Can we quantify what can be forgiven? If the offender or the inflictor of pain asks for forgiveness, does this lessen one's suffering and facilitate forgiveness? And if someone asks for forgiveness, does this minimize the weight of their pain? Buddhists and Christians say that when a person forgives, a weight is lifted off their shoulders since sorrow and the desire for vengeance rest most of all on the shoulders of the subject, the victim. But how do we forgive cruelty that isn't human, but demonic? Or cruelty that is even more demonic because it is practiced by humans? Would Buddha forgive? Would Jesus?

But, if forgiveness is not possible and if it does not even cross the victim's mind to forgive his torturer, why does he forget? The forgetting of a person who has suffered immoderately must be different to that of someone who has suffered little and who is able to forgive. The mathematics of forgiving and forgetting. There is a forgiving-forgetting and there is a forgetting that will never forgive. The English language should put an end to this link between forgiving and forgetting, or between forgetting and faith. Forgetting is a reverse remembering. It needn't have anything to do with forgiveness.

Olvido, in Spanish, and also in Portuguese, relates to the act of leveling, homogenizing. It also pertains to the religious concept of forgiveness, but it is more mundane, secular. In this case, memory resembles a rough topography and forgetting is like a steam roller, which flattens mountain ranges and hills and levels the continent that is memory. Forgetting is a grinder, a chainsaw, a blender, a powerful electric mixer. All of the obstacles in the mnemonic relief are smoothed out. Enter a brain full of forgetting and the landscape will be flat, clear, an open field across which you can see far into the distance. But see what? What does one see in a brain leveled out by forgetting? The subterranean world of this plain is always simmering and on the verge of boiling. Tread carefully. The inventers of words must have thought there was something such as an integrated and definitive forgetting, a mythological and divine forgetting. They have forgotten the men who, when wracked with pain, create a tumultuous forgetting. God may eventually forget. Man needs to remember to forget, to remember in order to be able to forget. His forgetting is not smooth; it is rough and full of lumps, because his forgetting was beaten with an old mixer.

Perhaps the best word to denote the kind of forgetting experienced by a victim of torture is *lethargy*. This forgetting is a kind of death, not a kind of leveling out, or of forgiveness. A deep slumber and apathy which allows the person to continue living. Without this memory of death, the victim will be unable to live, or will only be able to do so with the infinite memory of pain. He will then become a whole other kind of victim—the victim of memory. How can the tortured remember without being victimized all over again? Is it perhaps a matter of time?

TATTOO

The number on her arm is A 16.334. The Jewish prisoners who were labeled "A" were captured in May of 1944. There were a total of 20,000 men and 29,354 women. Of these women, she was number 16,334. When her daughter visited the Holocaust Museum, Yad Vashem, in Jerusalem in 2010, in search of her mother's diary, which is kept there, the museum's director stumbled upon a register of the people who worked in the kitchens of Auschwitz in 1944. It had been written by a Nazi officer and contained her name and number, as well as those of many of her peers.

The effect of seeing that number on her arm, now so much a part of her body and of the composition of her figure that no one even notices it anymore, is altogether different to the effect of seeing her name and number written in the camp register, jotted down by a Nazi officer. The daughter feels as if she were seeing it for the first time. As if she had not known her mother had a number tattooed on her arm or that she had been a prisoner. This story, which had been told to the daughter throughout her childhood—at home, in the living room, in the kitchen—was also in official documents? It really happened? Everything they'd been told—until then only real in the imaginations of those who'd heard it and of those who remember living it—also once had a dimension, a size, and a volume in the hands of a soldier? In the hands of the soldier who wrote down her name and number?

When Mother saw the register, with her name recorded there, she was not shaken; she rarely is. The museum director warned the two daughters to be careful when showing this to her.

The daughter took due care, but in the end, it wasn't necessary. Her mother refuses to be perturbed, or perhaps she simply was not perturbed. For those to whom these things effectively happened, they simply happened. They are facts, not fabulations. Yes, this is how it happened. What can this piece of paper add to what she already knows, to what she already lived?

Her tattoo is not a cause for self-pity. She wears her tattoo neither with pride or shame. It is simply there, a part of her. If someone offered her the chance to have it removed, she wouldn't. She doesn't insist on remembering, but she also doesn't want to excise this physical mark of her time there. Memory may forget, but the body informs and recalls and this is a mark she wants to retain.

Her skin has grown flaccid, wrinkled, and the number has wrinkled with her. The color is fading; once purple, it is now blue. The number has grown old with her. But, in a way, in this number, she is still there, in 1944: she is still nineteen years old, she is still Yugoslavian, she still speaks another language, and she has just arrived at the camp. When her daughter looks at that number, she sees her mother with the eyes she has now, which are of a near-absolute innocence, and tries to imagine how those eyes must have seemed when she first arrived at the camp, certain that she had lost her mother. She sees her eyes searching around her, observing her surroundings, and tries to picture her expression. She imagines a mixture of resignation, and a little curiosity. Did she cry? She has never seen her mother cry, nor has her sister, though she has seen her father cry many times. Did they take away her tears, or has she simply never cried? For those who were tattooed, is everything just a fact? Do occurrences cease to be frightening, after they are assigned a number? Do they simply become facts of life? *I became really tough, didn't I? I think it's because I didn't care whether I lived or died. Sometimes, we would even ask the Germans to kill us.*

Since she was a kid, the daughter has imagined what it must be like to have a number on your arm. *Mom, how did they make the number stay forever? They branded us like cattle—with a needle that pricks your skin.*

These days, almost everyone gets tattooed. And people have been tattooing themselves forever. In prison, tattoos have various meanings and have become a kind of language. Prisoners use tattoos to communicate. For the religious, no matter their belief, tattoos have a sacrificial value and are seen as a way of surrendering one's body to a divinity. Pain is necessary; not in the sense that it is inevitable, but as part of the sacrificial process. The sign of surrender, of abandon, of fidelity to a group is inscribed onto the body of the faithful subject, and symbolized in the tattoo. In the poem "The Great Mystical Circus," Jorge de Lima writes of Margarete, the acrobat who tattooed on herself the passion of Christ. The boxer, Rudolph, possessed her, despite the tattoo, which stopped any other men from approaching her. After penetrating her, he converted to Christianity and died. Out of this, were born the two purest girls of the mystic circus; girls who would perform naked and could levitate without resorting to tricks. From tattooed purity and converted vice was born total purity. Purity is even purer because it is associated with pain because the pain is literally felt in the flesh. Religious pain cleanses the body of mundane temptations and is even able to clean the unbeliever's impurities.

Today's tattoo fad seems to have various meanings: the mark of belonging to a group; resistance toward the clean, stainless body of the traditional bourgeoisie (even though the bourgeois are the ones tattooing themselves); a cautious rite of passage through pain; or maybe it's just a fad, with no real meaning at all.

Mother jokes, *Look, I have a tattoo, too!*

Tattooing oneself willingly might also be a way of celebrating those who were coerced to do so. If this is the case and if these cases do indeed exist, we are faced once again with the idea of sacrifice. To sacrifice oneself in the name of those who suffered, as a physical reminder of evil, seems ridiculous. Even so, her daughter is (and has always been) attracted to this idea, and to the idea itself of sacrifice. To sacrifice oneself as a way of resisting a general tendency toward adaptation, toward choosing the easiest route. Her daughter loves to be a hero.

In the industrial machine that was Nazism, tattoos were chosen for their efficiency and because they branded indelibly, but also because they humiliated the prisoners. Primo Levi wrote of how prisoners who were branded with smaller numbers would laugh at prisoners with larger numbers, who would face numerous problems before they learned how to act appropriately inside the camp.

When her daughter was in Poland, in 2009, she spent Shabat with Polish Jews. They had dinner in a hall near the synagogue and, during dinner, an Israeli Jew, some sort of clandestine professional in Warsaw, asked her what she was doing in Poland. She answered that she was going to visit Auschwitz, where her mother had been a prisoner. To him, someone who lived in Poland, and who had the typical, pragmatic personality of an Israeli, this was no novelty.

He asked, *Did your mother have a number?* The daughter said *Yes.* To which he responded, *Very good!*

Nowadays, a person might feel proud or boastful of their tattooed numbers. She has a number, therefore she truly suffered. When her daughter was young, she would tell her schoolmates that her mother had a number tattooed on her arm. She doesn't do this anymore. But people will ask, when they find out her mother is a survivor, *Does she have a number?* The daughter will nod. They feel perplexed. The number is a mark of torture. Those who were tortured in the Brazilian military dictatorship are also ashamed of showing people their marks, and people feel bewildered when they see them. Marks affect truth, even though truth is also to be found in those it did not visibly mark.

In Kafka's *In the Penal Colony*, a machine that is both divine and demonic writes the convicted person's sentence on their body. These people, in turn, can be convicted for infractions that are of no apparent importance. In the novel, for example, a prisoner will be submitted to this inscription simply because he has fallen asleep during his shift. And so the machine inscribes on his body something along the lines of "You must respect your superiors." The machine pierces the skin while also carefully cleaning off the blood, ensuring a hygienic process. After the first six hours of physical suffering, the prisoner has entered a state of torpor and pleasure, and will start mentally and physically reading into the significance of his sentence, which will make him feel an unspeakable pleasure. In the end, he dies and is thrown in a nearby valley. The machine's creator is a former commander who now has only one follower, a man who venerates him as if he were an actual god.

He keeps his incomprehensible drawings, and he programs the machine so that it executes its role to perfection, tattooing the sense of the sentence onto the body of the prisoner.

The Nazis did not tattoo the prisoners' infractions on their bodies; instead they tattooed the ineffaceable reminder that they were indeed prisoners. This both facilitated the Nazis' work and also inscribed on the prisoners' skin their greatest and only infraction—existing. What is written on the body—wrinkles, for example, and flab, but most of all tattoos—both gain and give to the person the meaning of their existence. She exists because she has this mark and she has this mark because she exists.

Mom, do you know what the "A" in your tattoo means?

I do. It stands for "Auschwitz." No, that's not it. I know. It means Arbeit: *work.*

HUMILIATION

Before the war, because my parents were religious, I couldn't carry my book bag on Saturdays. And everyone made fun of me because of it. I felt so humiliated. I think humiliation is the worst feeling. Or maybe it's that I just accepted things the way they were. I was a conformist. Sometimes I think I suffered more before the war than during it.

Maybe she didn't feel as humiliated before the war because there was no way of imagining or even pondering that one individual could be blamed for everything that was happening. When external evil is so clear and the punishment suffered so collective, the humiliation felt decreases. Before the war, she must have thought that it was her fault: she belonged to a religious family and was different from all her schoolmates. Her friends laughed at her and she felt humiliated. Humiliation is also connected to the solitude of the ridiculed. The greater the solitude, the greater the feeling of humiliation. When suffering is shared, this suffering becomes increasingly located in the other. There must also be a retrospective perception of humiliation, far in the future from all that was suffered. After having lived through the war, she compares her feelings of humiliation. We, in the future, cannot imagine a greater humiliation than losing our parents to murder, or having a number tattooed on our arm; than hunger, thirst, or cold; than punishment. But those who have lived through it all can conceive of greater humiliations. And, to her, having been laughed at might indeed be a greater humiliation.

The feeling of humiliation must also be closely related to vanity;

the individual becomes ridiculous, laughable in the eyes of the community to which he wants to belong. Because the Jews, and other prisoners, did not want to belong to the Nazi community, perhaps, because of this, they were able to feel at least marginally less humiliated. They could be consoled by the small sense of humanity that they still held onto, by saying, "If they want to humiliate me, it is because they are inferior to me." The prisoners were humiliated in their humanity, but not in their individuality. Except, as Mother says, even though they knew the attack on them wasn't individual, but collective—which was a relief in a way—even then, they had no way of reacting, and were forced to conform. To be what the humiliators wanted them to be. To conform. To become the shape of the other's desire, even against their will. This is also a penetrating, bruising kind of humiliation. A more oblique kind of humiliation. As if the executioner were to say, *You may feel, or even know, that you're superior to me, but you can't do anything, and this proves that you're inferior. If you really were superior, you would react; but you are so abject, you can't even do that. And all this confirms the need for you to be truly humiliated.* The logic of evil is vicious when practiced in such a physical and individualized way; there is no way of escaping it. The Nazis took care of each and every individual they persecuted. Their destruction was massive and collective, but it was also small and individual. Every Jew, gypsy, and homosexual had to be killed. Every one of them had to feel intimately persecuted and guilty about their identity and, in this way, there was no way of reacting, because the method was precisely to destroy individuality, to destroy any shadow of their identity so that they could then accuse them of not having resisted.

You don't resist, you don't react. You deserve to be treated the way we're treating you.

One day, the daughter heard the statement, *The Germans never forgave the Jews for the Holocaust.* This is true and must have been the case not only with every soldier, but also with the entire structure of Nazism. It is the opposite of Nelson Rodrigues' phrase, "*te perdoo por te trair*"—"I forgive you for betraying you"—a verse that Chico Buarque also sings, and could be more aptly expressed as: "I do not forgive you for having hurt you." Following in this imponderable logic of humiliation and evil, the soldiers must all have thought: *Why are you making me go through the humiliation of humiliating you, you vile and vain creature, when you're not worth even that? You're so abject you won't even react to my provocations; why are you forcing me to sink so low to attack you? I do this because you are forcing me to, and I won't forgive you for it, and so I will humiliate you even more.* And the Nazis as a whole must have also felt similarly. *It is the Jews, purulent and insignificant as they are, who have forced our hand in this war, and compelled us to do something that is unworthy of the great history of Germany.*

She is a conformist to this day. She will not argue or disagree, but instead asks to change the subject or says, *It doesn't matter, everything is fine.* This will sometimes annoy her daughters. That said, they aren't able to explicitly disagree with each other, either. They might disagree, but then they simply choose to stop discussing the matter. They prefer to simply resort to a *Nevermind.*

This is both good and bad (as most things are). The daughters still live under their mother's regime of conformity and acceptance, which justifies and lends significance to the difficulty they feel in fighting or even disagreeing. Under this regime, arguments are not really important, nothing is of much importance when it is done in the name of a family and a sorority whose union locates itself in their mother's name, experience, and being. Why argue? Nothing is more important than the fact that we are alive and well. But, at the same time, the absence of arguments and discussions feeds into deeper, quieter disagreements, which might in turn take root. Her daughter has always felt envious of families that argue, of sisters who swear at each other, speak the truth, and are then able to talk to each other as if nothing had happened. The fact that they don't argue in the open feels to her like a flaw, or a defect.

Conformity, on the other hand, can also be a kind of resistance. You want me to resist and to react, so I don't. I will conform to what you want me to be and this will make you even angrier, angrier than if I had reacted, because if I had reacted, you would have had every right to attack me. If I conform, by attacking me, you show yourself to be even more perverse. There is a wise, inverted perversity in conformity, which her and her daughters ascribe to. By accepting and overcoming their disagreements (at least on the surface), the conformist is able to exert even greater power. Conformity is also a kind of power; conformists should not be deceived.

But she does not merely conform. She also accepts. Acceptance and conformity are two very different things. Conformity secretly contains a more tactical, unassuming power. Not acceptance—acceptance is truthful. She accepts. She accepts that life is also suffering, that things do not always go the way she'd like them to, that death exists, and that it is impossible to know what will happen from one second to the next. When she is contradicted, by people or by life, she is above resignation, even though she always eventually surrenders. She knows this is just the way things are; they are almost never the way they should be. *It is good when nothing happens.* Because she knows that if something happens, it can be bad. It upsets her daughters, though, that she does not know how to deal with good things and also does not know how to praise her daughters, her grandchildren—or anyone at all. The fear she feels that something good might happen is palpable; the fear that pride or self-praise will bring something bad. *But Mom, why would something good bring something bad? Why would luck, good fortune, and success, bring bad luck?* She doesn't answer. Her superstitions—which are numerous, much greater than her daughters can begin to imagine—are so deep-rooted they keep her from talking about them. That's just the way it is and there's nothing to be said about it. Best not to defy fate, and to feel pride for the good as you would for the things you scorn. Fate is always on the lookout for the good, keeping watch so that it can stop it from being victorious. Good only exists to remind us of the existence of evil. This is why it is best not to brag when something good happens. Best to keep it quiet, and to be more attentive.

She accepts suffering, but fears luck. To her, suffering is more certain and is bound to happen.

Her daughters inherited from her a deep sense of humiliation. Not a Christian sense of humiliation, where it is thought that through humiliation one experiences the worst and is therefore deserving of paradise. It is difficult to explain a side of humiliation that is not fully negative. It is humiliation in the broad sense of the word: to become like the dust from which we've come, to know deeply that no one is worth a thing. To know that, by humiliating oneself, or by letting oneself be humiliated, a person is simply becoming what she is, fundamentally: dust, dirt, a chemical compound of matter and words.

FORGETTING

A train. A father. A mother. A brother. A mad aunt. Two young nephews. A coat that is too short to hide her nephews. Two knees. A stone. There. Everything is forgotten. Her memory is brimming and ready to forget.

THE WORD

Mom, if you had to remember one of the words they used to say at the camp, which would it be? Achtung *and* Zählappell. *Those are the only two I can remember. You don't remember any other words? No, none. Is that all you wanted to know?*

Her daughter grows annoyed. How can she possibly not remember any other words if she was there for eleven months? Not the officers' words, nor the prisoners', nor the ones she must have thought herself. Why does she not remember words, when there is nothing more important? How can she ask her daughter if that's all she wants to know, as if it were so little? She's embarrassed that her diary is going to be published because she thinks it is not literary and she knows her daughter's book will be very literary. There's no comparison, her mother thinks. How can that diary, which is so simple, so sparse of words, be printed side by side with her daughter's impressions, her daughter who is so careful about how things are said? She doesn't understand that this is precisely what her daughter wants. She is embarrassed by the words she remembers because they are not at the same level as her daughter's complex thoughts. What must it be like for her to have a daughter who works with words? Does this make her feel more embarrassed, proud, fearful, or was it precisely her mother's words and non-words that led her daughter to choose this, words, as her profession? In the end, her daughter is trying to say what she herself did not want to, or could not say. Her mother has authorized these words to be uttered now, in whichever way her daughter desires.

But how can she choose words her mother can't even remember? The daughter can't help wondering if she would have remembered more if she had been there herself. This thought is another unjustified trespass in the many that transpire in the kidnapping and appropriation of her mother's words. She must steal from her mother's and father's lives in order to sustain their survival. To be where they were, in their place, is a ridiculous fantasy, and yet it is also inevitable; it's a fanciful notion, a whim, but it is also a kind of redemption. The desire to salvage some of the suffering that has already been lived.

Achtung means attention. *Zählappell,* roll call. Attention, in English as in Portuguese, *atenção*, is an appeal for a person to be more careful, to look around more, to concentrate, but it also denotes the care we take with other people, a lingering gaze, or an affectionate gesture. But not in German. *Achtung*, in German, under those specific conditions, means *That's forbidden! Don't do that!* It is a false warning, which hides a restriction: if you do this, you will be punished. But what difference does it make if the prisoner would be punished anyway, even if he weren't to do it? Why pay it any attention? And why bother issuing the warning? How difficult it is to understand the logic of fear that roots itself in language, to understand why language aggravates a fear that is both before and beyond it. If the soldier did not say *achtung*, as if it were a shield, would the prisoner perhaps feel calmer? But if he does, it is best to be on guard. The daughter doesn't understand any of it. How would she react to an *achtung* that, in the end, means nothing? The daughter can't stand words that mean nothing. She dredges up the meaning of every traffic sign;

leans on every word's etymology in order to better understand it, and meticulously explains it, until she finds in it a possible poetry.

Zählappell was the call Nazis would make several times a day under the pretext of verifying that all the numbers added up, that all the morning prisoners were the same as the evening prisoners, that no one was asleep, had gone missing, escaped, fallen ill, or died.

Attention and *roll call* are the only two words she remembers from eleven months of terror. As if the concentration camp had been a classroom. Pay attention to the roll call.

If her daughter had to try to think of the words that best summed up her mother, they would be, *What says what?* which is what she says when she is trying to remember something she has forgotten. It's her way of saying, *What was I trying to say? Fiff* is how she pronounces *fifth*. *Steer wheel* is *steering wheel*. *What is the new?* instead of *What's new?* She transforms everyday words and questions into music. If someone says they want to eat, she sings: *An apple a day keeps the doctor away!* To this day she hasn't been able to say *son of a gun*. She says *sons of the guns*. When someone cut her off in traffic, back when she still drove, she would exclaim: *Sons of the guns.* It is the worst she can bring herself to say.

In the last few years, she has grown more and more silent. During family reunions, she will sit, staring; sometimes at nothing, sometimes at people. Sometimes, she'll exclaim, *All of this came from me!*

As Mother stood under the *chuppah* at her granddaughter's wedding, it was impossible not to think: this woman, who has survived the war, is now standing here watching her granddaughter get married. Where has history gone? How were these paths trodden?

What must it feel like to have been there, and to now be here? What is the path memory draws through those two places? As she sits in silence, she gives the impression that these are the thoughts that must be going through her head. Eyes that see more than words can describe how absurd—if only slightly—this change of fate is. How can one life encompass two such distinct possibilities? What words can be used to describe this? *Achtung* and *Zählappell?* Where are these words now? What mouths are they in, why are they being said, what words can we say, and what are the words she can remember, including those she has forgotten?

What words has she forgotten?

One day, her mother, who loves to imagine hypothetical situations, asked her daughter over the phone, *What are the blind men dreaming?* At first, the daughter couldn't understand. It sounded as if she were asking about specific blind men in a specific situation who were dreaming something at that precise moment. She added: *Yes! What are they dreaming, if they can't see? How are they seeing images in dreams?* And this is when her daughter understood what she was asking, having recalled that her mother often mixed up the present continuous with the simple present. *What are the blind men dreaming?* was actually *What do the blind dream?* And yet, in some unexpected and surprisingly beautiful way, that sentence, in its suspension of time and its displacement of grammar and syntax, in its fully autonomous meaning, independent from any narrative logic, synthesized precisely her mother's way of being-in-the-world. As if she were herself stuck in the present continuous, in an eternal state of becoming, filled with wonder by the possibilities of the world, of nature. There was war, there was exile, suffering—everything. But this past, which took place and cannot be denied, though it is perhaps forgotten, confuses itself in her memory with an eternal inclination toward the present, where there is no perfect mastery of grammar, but a disconnected sense of appropriation, in which the perception of things matters more than the things themselves.

LIFE

If the daughter could speak, she'd say: *Mom, do you know what it means to be alive? Being alive is an organic composition of substances so very miniscule they are absurd.*

WRITING

Everyone around me, with me, is full of sadness. Unfortunately, we know what lies ahead. Papa has been sitting on the ottoman all morning, he stares straight ahead and says nothing. From time to time he sighs deeply, glances over at us, and shuts his eyes. Mama comforts us; she is not one to believe in evil but she is readying things, packing up the book bags, baking cakes, and at moments, in secret so no one can see, she, too, sighs briefly.

Mother never had any interest in writing. She thinks she writes poorly. And yet, as soon as she arrived in Sweden, and was quarantined, she found a notebook, wrote in it "My Diary," and started penning her most recent memories. It's possible she didn't have much else to do and, almost certainly, that these memories were so strong, she felt she had to write them down. But this was a necessity she had never felt, and never felt again.

She claims she doesn't have a good grasp on writing, on language, but she writes about the past in the present tense, as a writer would. In resorting to this device, she lends greater strength to the sense of reality and drama in the text. Why does she tell the story of her imprisonment in the present? Where does this unexpected literary awareness come from? The diary isn't narrated fully in the present; only some parts are. When they speak together in Portuguese, the daughter notices how her mother mixes up the tenses, using some inadequately and speaking the language more so by habit and intuition than through any sort of linguistic awareness. Throughout the process of translating the diary, she also found it very difficult to translate verb tenses. In any case, the effect of using the present tense in the first part of the diary, is quite beautiful. It changes everything. *Everyone around me, with me, is full of sadness.* All of this had taken place only one year before she wrote this sentence. It was recent and, at the same time, perhaps it was as distant in time as anything could be. The use of the present tense can be due both to proximity and distance, as if she were glimpsing a scene from afar, in the long lost movie theater of her memory and—like much of what she would later come to tell—as if it all hadn't quite happened to her, but to another "her" that she observed from afar. To a third person of herself, which her daughter has chosen to emphasize in this book, in this looted post-account.

The daughter, and probably all those who read these lines, cannot help picturing this familial scene, which took place on the day before their capture, with the full knowledge that the Germans would be coming to take them. *All sad.* What is the imminence of this anticipation? Is it an anticipation for the moment they will become the prisoners of a foreign apprehender—for reasons unknown to them—and taken to a foreign place—that is also unknown—and deprived of everything they own, all of which will most likely end in death? How could she be baking sweets? She consoles her children, does not believe in evil, and sighs when no one can see her.

The present tense also reinforces the force of this imminence. Heightening the sense that their apprehenders could arrive at any moment. Even as we are reading the text.

WILL

They escorted [us] to a plain old pigsty which we, ourselves, cleaned and brought in clean, cold sand. We spent nine days in that pigsty. Papa became very sick, a high fever. My grandmother also got a cold. She was frail. Mama kept her strength up but you could see it on her. She always had an eye on us and did what she could to ease things for us. Nothing hurt her, she didn't feel the ordeal for herself.

During a recent trip Mother went on with her daughter and granddaughter, she once again repeated the phrase that could have served as her life motto, an anthem her daughters found both oppressive and liberating: *You can do anything. You just have to want it. It's all in the mind.* During this trip, for what must have been the thousandth time, her daughter argued with her. She tried to explain that not everything was in the mind and that there are things that cannot be willed. She tried to convince her that, for example, when it comes to depression, there are certain things that are unconscious and that, as much as the depressed person might want to be well, they cannot be held singularly responsibly for their recovery, lest this leave them even more vulnerable. She nods, only resignedly accepting her daughter's reasoning. But she doesn't agree. She thinks depression is no more than a flight of fancy and doesn't understand how a person can become depressed for no apparent reason, or at least without a clear reason. *There must be a reason for someone to be sad.* Seen from this point of view, melancholy can seem almost chimeric, like a luxurious invention.

As the daughter reads her mother's diary, and the account she is writing about her, it becomes easier to understand what until then had seemed to her no more than a matter of obstinacy. When confronted with psychological suffering, it's possible that the will—the will for potency, will as a stronger engine than desire itself—does not have the power to keep the body and soul from suffering. In everyday life, we cannot and should not ask that the individual bear the responsibility for easing or even curing their own suffering. This is unsustainable and would only increase the person's sense of pain and guilt.

But confronted with suffering that is unspeakable and unbeatable, where the motivations are clearly external, perhaps it is then possible to attribute a super-human quality to the will. Perhaps, in these situations, everything really does depend on the strength of a person's will and in their ability to say, *You just have to will it.* This must be the source of the apparent negligence with which she treated her husband's constant state of depression, as well as her daughter's own bouts of depression—always as if it were a feebleness that she could only accept with a certain reservation.

The daughter also suffers from this prejudice—both good and bad—though without her mother's motivations. Her kids always complain that she doesn't pay attention to them when they are hurt, always downplaying the pain they claim to be feeling; that she always says, *Get up, it'll get better soon.*

Her mother never complains about anything. Not even when she's in great pain. If she calls for help it's because the problem must be very serious and the physical pain unbearable. But never mental pain. It's hard to tell if she even feels this kind of pain.

Mom, don't you ever feel lonely, sad, or depressed? her daughter asks. And she says that yes, she does sometimes feel lonely, but that loneliness is normal for someone her age. And she explains that when that happens, she'll simply watch television, read a book, or go out with her friends, and that the loneliness she had been feeling passes. *But what about sadness and depression?* To which she replies: *Why should I feel sad? I have everything I want. I have a good life.* Her daughter understands everything she says and yet nothing at all.

To Mother, hiding pain is a matter of pride. Once, when she saw how upset her daughter was because her boyfriend had left her, she felt almost embarrassed by how explicitly she exhibited feelings of jealousy: *It's ugly to show weakness; you have to hide your jealousy. Once, I saw the boy I liked going out with another girl. I hid, I was so hurt, but I never showed a thing.*

Her father was the exact opposite. He liked to show off his pain; to dramatize, expand, and transform it in his stories. He suffered because of what he had lived and because of what he hadn't lived; he suffered for no reason at all, or at least no apparent reason. He said he had realized that *love doesn't exist. It's abstract, a fantasy.* For Mother, love was concrete: love was baking sweets, hiding your pain, consoling your children, and sweeping the sand off the dirty floor.

FIXED MEMORY

She always remembers the same things. If we try to get her to remember something other than the stories she always tells, she can't. Her daughter tries to catch her unaware, out of the blue; she tries to engineer free, unprecedented associations, but nothing comes of it, or at least almost nothing. It's as if her memory were fixed. As the daughter reads her mother's diary, she notices that the stories she tells are the ones written there. The memories she wrote in her diary are probably fixed memories. Or more accurately, they have become fixed because she wrote them.

What would've happened if she hadn't written a diary? Would everything have vanished, like all those memories she didn't write down? Possibly. Where and what are those things that she lived and then forgot? Were there other things, too, worse things, funnier things, or more particular things? Nothing, nothing. No words or scenes, no gestures or habits. There is a void where her memories should be. Her stories are so fixed that it sometimes seems as if they weren't memories at all, but lists and impersonal facts. They are there, ready to be told, if necessary.

It is as if all she had written at that moment, in Sweden, was done to consolidate and solidify time, to solidify her recollections. And so these recollections became future-less: solid, indissoluble, unmodified even by dreams, time, or emotion. Nothing can dilute what has been massively closed off in that memory.

And why does her daughter insist that there be other memories? Why does she insist that the stories Mother has told be complemented by nuance, surprise—the unknown? As if it were possible for her to recapture those situations that have slipped away and—because they are swift and have disappeared—might reveal something behind or outside the fixedness of Mother's memory, something that might allow her to better understand the chasm that separates her from her mother. But it is precisely this something that is missing. It cannot be suppressed. There is no way of making memory more flexible, suppler, or more fluid, and to make new facts appear. Her memory is a black box sinking in the ocean.

DESIRE

Today a guy complimented me for the first time. I felt myself blush. Months and days of suffering have passed and I looked at myself in the mirror for the first time. How do I look? I can't believe I've been complimented, that I'm pretty. Am I a pretty young lady now? He can't have meant it, not when my hair is like this. I look like a man, with my short hair, and so thin. I keep looking at myself in the mirror, combing my hair, looking at my eyes and at my white teeth, which I think are the best parts of me. I was preoccupied and I didn't realize he was watching me. "I've been here for a while. You're pretty. Will you let me get to know you?" I was very confused, even my ears turned red, I jumped out of bed and said "I don't want anything to do with you, leave me alone, please," and rushed away. I don't know why I don't want anything to do with him (I speak to my buttons). It's true I get along with him; so, why not?

Men liked her—a lot. There was the German singer who courted her on her way back to Yugoslavia, after the war, and then there was Juro, the one she mentions in her diary. He was a Yugoslav soldier, not a Jew. When she arrived in her home town, Senta, she found that she'd received a letter from her old boyfriend before the war, asking her to marry him and join him in Israel. Juro also wanted to marry her, but her brother, who had also survived the war and was in Senta at the time, didn't let her marry Juro because he wasn't Jewish. Her brother went to the United States, which was another reason she decided not to meet up with her old boyfriend—she wanted to go with him. But she never did and she never again spoke with Juro, nor with her old boyfriend, Moishe.

Instead she went to Brazil.

After her husband's death, she tried to find Moishe, but to no avail.

Not only did her brother forbid her from marrying one of her suitors because he wasn't Jewish, he also took her identity papers and passed them off as belonging to his girlfriend, a fourteen-year-old Polish girl. This meant she wasn't able to leave Senta and go to the United States, or even anywhere else, and forced her to go after a third suitor, in Hungary, so that she could obtain some form of identification. This is the one she finally married.

The photos of her from then and the number of suitors she had are evidence of how beautiful she was. After looking into a mirror for the first time in a long while—they certainly didn't have mirrors in the concentration camps—she asked herself, *Am I a pretty young woman now?* Because she just couldn't believe all the compliments she was getting.

Soon after, Mother wonders, in her diary, about how she could possibly have started worrying about her weight so soon, after having gone hungry for so long, and comments on how she decided to start exercising every day to stay in shape.

How does the process of recovering one's image, and the desire to be pretty, which she still feels strongly today, come about? How does a person who didn't care if she died, for whom life and death had made little difference, start caring so quickly about beauty, about the possibility of seduction?

Of course, a lack of distinction between the genders must have been one of the first consequences of the prisoners' dehumanization, even though their roles were often separate in the camp.

Only women worked in the kitchen and they (more so than the men) were probably the ones responsible for mending clothes, stripping their clothes so that they wouldn't become lice-ridden, and other domestic, painstaking tasks. Perhaps, even in the most grotesque kind of suffering, the kind for which there is no end or clear target, gender differences still exist. The Germans were taught not to humiliate women through sexual violence. No. Their kind of machine-like conscience—both correct and fully ideological—did not leave room for this kind of sexual activity, which in the end would not serve to humiliate the Jews but the Germans themselves, who would have had to sink low enough to do so. The prisoners' humiliation was engineered through the loss, in both the men and the women, of their sexual environment, and of desire itself.

But desire swiftly reasserts itself, at least in her case, and in the same dimensions as before, or perhaps with even more force, if one takes into account all the men who expressed interest in her throughout her journey home.

It is as if this manifestation of desire were a sign of the restoration of humanity; of each person's confidence in the possibility of their existence as more than just beings, in the possibility of leading an integral and integrated existence.

After her husband's death, she showed such willingness to try to find her first boyfriend that it seemed as if she'd been thinking of him for a long time. What had happened to him? Had he survived? She searched for his name at the Holocaust Museum in Jerusalem and placed notices in the Israeli newspaper. She didn't get an answer and gave up quickly, just as she had given up on her romantic involvement with Juro (without ever really under-standing why). It was as if she had been obeying some external command (fate) and her own desire was disobeying that command. The fact that she didn't immediately find her first ex-boyfriend simply meant, to her, that she was not meant to find him, or that by finding him, she might be running the risk of thwarting some coded law that only reveals itself through impediments.

To her, impediments are more certain than good fortune, good omens, or serendipity. When things go poorly, or do not go well, it is clear to her that fate has had its way; that it was not challenged, and that an individual will did not manifest itself. On the other hand, when a desire is ostensibly fulfilled, or when a person feels happy because of something that has happened, the risks are many. Everything can (and ultimately will) collapse, just as it has many times before. It is better, therefore, to err on the side of caution, thereby avoiding the bad, as well as the good, which is sometimes even worse.

Many years later, in 2011, her daughter decided she'd try again to find her mother's first boyfriend, Moishe Schick. Following this obsessive and voracious impulse, she was able to find reference in the Holocaust Museum's digital archive to a certain Rachel Schick, who was originally from Senta and had died in Auschwitz in 1944. There, she also found a document that listed the name of the last person to have conducted this search: Moishe Schick. It was him. That night, the daughter dreamt about the possibil-ity of their reunion. She wrote to the museum, and to various other establishments, in an attempt locate him. The next day, she received a response from the museum. When Moishe Schick had searched for his sister, in 1955, he had told them that he was living in a kibbutz near Jerusalem. The daughter called the kibbutz and asked to speak to him. The attendant who answered the phone, an older woman, said: *Moishe Schick? He died a long time ago! In 1983. Probably of cancer. Does he have any relatives? Yes, a daughter, Shlomit.* And she gave her her number. The daughter immediately called her mother. *He died,* she said. *Ah, I told you. I knew it. Do you want me to call his daughter? What for? To see if she knows anything about you. No! He probably never mentioned me to her.*

In this way, oscillating between the negation and the affirmation of her desire—yet with the knowledge that its negation would always be guaranteed—she is able to construct for herself a much more affirmative identity than she may have otherwise. When she heard about Moishe's death, she said, *Yes, such is life.* There is no way of knowing what happened then, in the most intimate corner of her being, a place to which perhaps not even she has access and which immediately led her to call her daughter and say: *If you're curious and want to call his daughter, you can.* It seems that she is indeed able to satisfy her own desires, that is, when she is able to locate that same desire in another. When she really wants to eat something, for example, she'll ask, *Do you want ice cream?* And in that moment, everyone will know she wants ice cream.

Her daughter called Shlomit, Moishe's daughter. She said to her: *Your father and my mother were sweethearts before the war. When she went back to her hometown, Senta, a letter was waiting for her, asking her to marry him.* Shlomit's reaction was as perplexed and enthusiastic as her own. She talks about how she, Shlomit, could have been Mother's daughter, and the daughter replies that she could have been her father's. They grow excited; they feel as if they had been sisters for a long time.

Soon afterwards, as she tells her mother about this conversation, with the same level of expectation and excitement she had shared with Shlomit, her mother reacts brusquely: *It's not him! There were two Moishe Schicks. This is the other one. It's not him, not at all.* The daughter is alone. She sits on a bench in the street and all of a sudden begins to cry.

Why does the daughter require so much fabrication, and what for? Is it possible to live outside these stories? Why does the daughter need to make up stories to pass the time, to narrate this book, to feel alive? She is always surprised by the gap that exists between life and stories; she cannot help but think that both are almost the same and that what people refer to as the difference between fiction and reality, is no more than a matter of pragmatism, of convenience. And yet this so-called reality insists on establishing limits and affirming the absurdity of the edifice of fiction. How can't it be him? Same city, same age, same name. But now her mother has decided there is another Moishe Schick. By unearthing a story that has been buried for so long, and with almost complete success, is the daughter causing her mother pain? How? What's the point in the absurd happiness she feels at the thought of meeting the daughter of a boyfriend her mother hasn't seen in sixty years? Part of her feels that the book she's writing might actually be unnecessary, that it is just another fabrication which allows her to turn everything into a story so that she can feel more like a character than a person. In the end, the comfort her mother feels in the adequacy of the present, and of facts, may be similar to the comfort her daughter feels in doing the exact opposite: in never feeling satisfied with unassailable limits and gorging herself on stories.

The truth is that it isn't one thing or the other. Reality is not self-sufficient or categorical, nor is her daughter so whimsically fictional. It's quite probable that Shlomit *is* Moishe Schick's daughter, and that she must tread carefully along this road, which is a compound of fiction and reality. Almost everything in the memories of war survivors, due to the interference of time, distance, and forgetting, ends up being a mixture of facts and dreams.

LANGUAGE

Nazism incorporated into its discourse many of the ideals of the post-French Revolution bourgeoisie, who were romantic and also aware of their collective rights and duties: nation, social justice, and the defense of nature, liberty, and the common well-being. The difference—the most significant and most powerful difference—is that, in order for the Nazi-Fascist regime to achieve these objectives, they needed to exterminate the biggest obstacle facing their realization: impurities. In other words, Jews, the Roma, homosexuals, and the disabled. The justification was, ostensibly, noble as was the cause. But it was the means that most impassioned the people. The end was such that the means seemed reasonable, though tough, as is the case with all absolutist and totalitarian policies and practices. But Nazis were satisfied in the practical realization of the means. It was the means that contained pleasure and truth, on the one hand (for active Nazis), and on the other, fear and omission (for collaborationists).

At the entrance to Auschwitz hangs the infamous sign: "Work Liberates." Placed side by side, these two ideas, work and liberty, seem mad, but at the same time, they explain everything. The verb "to liberate" is employed intransitively. It does not indicate who is liberated; all that is said is that work liberates, as if this liberation were generalized and unconditional. Does it liberate the worker or the one worked for? No. Work, in itself, liberates. The mere act of working turns the working subject into a liberated subject. And then there is another agreement which regulates the verb "to liberate." What does it liberate one from? This isn't explained, either.

It is as if the subject who does not work were shackled to something from which he can only liberate himself through work. Liberate whom and from what? This doesn't matter. It liberates.

Beyond the paradox inherent in this motto, which hangs at the entrance to a concentration camp, there is also a deeper, more subterranean contradiction, which unifies the totalitarian idea that all dictatorial regimes indissolubly conflate the idea of work with that of liberty. It is imperative for the individual to view work as a noble activity, as something immanent, which he must necessarily do for himself, not for others. We work because it is good to work, because it is noble and justifiable in and of itself. Work liberates through the act itself of work, possibly even within a prison system. There cannot be liberty outside the realm of work, not even when the objectives could be met outside this realm. Liberty is not in achieving what we would achieve through work, but in the work itself. Work is absolute and intransitive. In this sense, work and liberty are synonyms, not each other's causes.

What's more, before Auschwitz was turned into an extermination camp, it had been a camp for political prisoners, not just Jewish, but also Polish. If the sign had been hanging then, too, this would mean that the incarcerator was, in a way, cynically telling the prisoner that only work would liberate them. As if the executioner were to say: *You will only be liberated from me if you work for me. The longer you are a prisoner, or the more you work, the more liberated you will be.*

This phrase encapsulates the linguistic madness of Nazism. The threat to language itself is much more long-lasting and incisive than any political regime, and lives on indefinitely. It is against this that we must fight. And maybe the best way to defuse this linguistic explosive, which leaves infinite fragments in the memories of a place and a people, is from the inside, through stories, books, testimonies, and a continuous, monotonous insistence.

The swastika, for example, an ancient Aryan symbol (from Sanskrit) that represents the idea of peace, well-being, and harmony—for centuries, geometry has served as the abstract translation of human values—was quickly incorporated and disseminated by the Nazis and by the majority of the German population, and used to symbolize racial purity and obedience to the *Führer*. The Germans were said to have come from the first Germano-Nordic Europeans or, perhaps even further back in time, from the pure Indio-Persian race. This ascendency was the greatest possible guarantee for the furtherance of Germany's social equality and well-being.

In one of the anthems of the Hitler Youth—and they probably do not differ much one from the other—they sang the following: "Our flag means more to us than death;" "We belong to the *Führer*;" "Hitler is our companion;" "We will fight for eternity;" "Onward, onward;" "The youth are the hope for the future."

Here, the individual is always surpassed; in this ideological sphere, individual lives are only valued as cogs in a larger, worthier, and future-oriented machine. Man, the I, and the now are of no importance. All that matters is (Aryan) mankind and the future. But more than the future—which is small in terms of totalitarian aspirations—it is eternity that is at stake. As if Hitler—and the German flag—lived on in the unattainable eternity of time, alone and in perpetuity, the sole possibility of total ethnic purity.

The flag means more than death. The language of anthems

and of rallies, the language of order and slogans is always that of a surrender to objects, to fetishes that take the place of, and are worth more than men. A flag is worth more than a life, a history, a family, or an experience; it is grandiose, collective, symbolic.

In the anthem, they sang (naturally, as a chorus), "We belong to the *Führer.*" This idea of belonging to a larger, homogenous group, over which there reigns a singular, paternal, and all-inclusive leader, must be one of the human soul's biggest consolations—at least for its more infantile parts—and one of its greatest substitutions for autonomy. To belong: to be heteronomous and have ostensibly grandiose ideas, to be saved, to sink into the mass and lose oneself; there must be nothing more comforting than this identity of collective surrender. To belong to the other, to a mentor for whom one is capable of dying; to belong to another who is translated into clear symbols, like the flag, the anthem, the swastika, the raised hand, the focused gaze, stiff legs, and a clear enemy. Names—how clean and comforting are the names of things! When everything has been named, doubts are annulled and schisms dissolved. There ceases to be a subjective mode, or a future conditional; only the indicative and the imperative exist. Things are what they are and the world makes sense, both morally and directionally. Everything moves forward; it marches, it tramples, because there is something up ahead that must be reached. The present is justified by the brilliant expectation of what awaits us in the future and the future opens itself up at each stage we accomplish in the present. Time is split into stages, and turned into a list where each phase, once realized, is marked off as executed, just one more step on the way to achieving the final goal.

Euthanasia and the Final Solution: two clear terms. Euthanasia: the name given to the assassination of carriers of Down syndrome, physical handicaps, or other deficiencies, whether German or otherwise. The Final Solution: one of Nazism's central projects, it entailed the complete extermination of European Jews. Euphemism is one of the many linguistic strategies used to pacify behavior, and to quickly and efficiently execute a regime's goals. The euphemism loses its rhetorical, attenuating characteristics and, finally stripped of any dissimulating connotations, becomes truth itself, fact, its own justification. Rooted in subjectivity and in action, the euphemism will take on a certain nobility, as evidenced in the words themselves: *euthanasia* (good death) and *solution* (a cure, a remedy). It becomes a truth that the existence of deformed creatures, sexual aberrations, the Roma, and Jews (who are not bound by nationality), are a sickness that must be eradicated from the German *corpus,* in the name of the people's wellbeing. Society is the body and its leader, the head that thinks for it and on its behalf. God, father, leader. Everything is justified, in harmony.

The will to fight. The term *will,* permeated with Nietzschean and Schopenhauerian philosophy (both used mistakenly by Nazism), was the Nazis' invocatory stronghold for the bellicose behavior they expected from the *Volk,* or *people,* another word that also entered their jargon. Action must move forward, without hesitation or fear, but with confidence or, more accurately, with faith in the leader, in the mission and in the solution: this is will. In Nietzsche, the will appears in the idea of the *will to power* and in Schopenhauer in the *world as will and representation.* But, in Nietzschean thought, the will is a kind of necessity that emanates from the Earth itself, from Time, and, therefore, from man, who is a temporal being. Man, as such, does not control will, but is "controlled" by it, in a dynamic that is necessarily contradictory and imperfect, but also potent and creative. However, the appropriation by Hitlerism of the concept of will was markedly different; theirs was one in which will was a voluntary choice and attitude, a path leading forward, devoid of threats and ambiguities whose exercise depended on the person's self-control. It is in this sense related to the word *fight*, not *power,* and its connotations are also completely different. The *will to power* is the immanent force that leads to creation and to action, even if it must be at the cost of symbolic destruction. The *will to fight* is an arbitrary decision of which destruction is a means. Fighting, in this case, becomes the realization of the will, as well as its success. This same idea is built into the concept of common sense as willpower; her own mother uses this term as a cure-all for any psychological or emotional problem. *All you need is will. You can do anything if you will it.* The use of this word casts blame on man for everything that befalls him, whether good or bad, and is therefore in line with the *Führer*'s desire to keep the people attentive and fearful. If a person fails, it is through lack of will and weakness of character. It appeals to the depths of a person's honor and divides life into success and failure or the presence and absence of will. From this point of view, nothing is worse than weakness, and the weak must be scorned by those who have the will to fight.

For Schopenhauer, from whom Nietzsche drew inspiration, *will* is also a metaphysical and inevitable force, the source not only of creation, but also of all human suffering. Here, the burden of will carries negative connotations. Nazism reversed this concept; in Nazism, will is always auspicious, responsible for the victory we glimpse in the future. It is not determined, but determining, and the only metaphysical force present in the world is that of the *Führer* himself, who takes the place of the will as it exists in Schopenhauer and Nietzsche. If there is any immanence in Nazism at all, it is the *Führer*, who is abstract, categorical, necessary, the German people's reason for existing.

The People or *Volk*: a variety of terms were used during the Nazi regime, each composed of the word for people, such as *volksgemeinschaft*, the people's community; *volksgrenadier*, the people's soldiers; *volkskrieg*, the people's war; *volkstumskampf*, combat, popular struggle; *volksdeutsche*, the pure German race; *volkskörper*, the body of the people; and many more, as well as a phrase Hitler used repeatedly in his speeches, "You are nothing, your people are everything." The word *Volk* originally comes from *Folk*. The word, *Folk*, originally referred to a naval crew or to a closed group of fighters. Then, it came to refer to the common people, to tribes, or a multitude. Only later did it come to denote a population, though always retaining the connotation of "common people." Its reiterative use during the Nazi regime returned it, on the one hand, to its original meaning (of war) and on the other, also reclaimed for it a positive connotation. The people therefore become a kind of army of men and women who are valued precisely because they are the common people (though also necessarily pure). What the Weimar Republic had elevated in the name of education and culture was, in turn, disdained by Nazism in favor of a more basic, aggressive, and "natural" attitude. To be part of the *Volk*, you simply have to be ethnically pure. It was the revenge of the *Volk* against high culture, deracination, cosmopolitanism, and miscegenation. The Nazi regime lifted the common man to power, making him an equal in the multitude of equals who serve a common cause. When analyzing the language of the Third Reich, Victor Klemperer writes of how in *Mein Kampf*, Hitler sees "military service [...] principally, indeed exclusively in terms of a training to achieve maximum physical potential."

Victor Klemperer also writes in his diary about a poster he saw at his university in 1933, the year Hitler came to power, which read, "When a Jew writes in German, he lies." Language also bends to those who use it. When language is spoken by a pure German, it is the truth. The same words used by a Jew become false. A magico-mystical understanding of language is in evidence here, where its transformation is seen as dependent on those who use it. The German language (and no other language) is truth and the exclusive property of the German people, and cannot be vilified by other people or races. The superiority of the German people, therefore, extends magically to their words, to sound, and to enunciation. The *Führer* has the power to grant language the status of truth and to those who speak it, the power of its utterance.

Klemperer also makes reference to two detectives of the Nazi police force, Clemens and Weser, known by the pseudonyms "the Hitter and the Spitter," who had hammered him on the head with Alfred Rosenberg's *Myth* while they asked him how he dared to read a book that was glorified by the regime. Clemens and Weser must have felt honored to have been recognized for their actions: hitting and spitting. The men, reduced to and recognized by their roles, seem to justify their own existence, even though (or principally because) their roles are to hit and spit. *If I am a spitter, I spit; if I am a hitter, I hit.* Names and roles help realize mankind's perverse and infantile desire to merge with reality and if by doing so they also receive social recognition, even better. Multiplicity and opposition are outside the scope of Nazism. Everything is clear and united. All things have one sense and one direction only—even personality. Human beings calmly begin to take their places as cogs in a larger machine; they are proud and so will try to execute their roles with precision and excellence. Existing is a functional activity and philosophy, faced with this perspective, loses its reason to exist. Seen in this light, human values are transformed, even though they might bear the same name, nation, people, rights, duties, justice; everything starts to magically take on new meaning. Same words, different connotations. This is one of Nazism's biggest achievements. In their drive to transform people's hearts and minds, even the prisoners, weakened in their ability to think, end up absorbing the Nazi agenda.

FICTION AND REALITY

It's common sense—and apparently also logical—to assert that fiction and reality are separate. Fiction is false and reality is true. Even so, a consensus has not been reached—not personal, philosophical, or epistemological—about the meaning of truth, even though many claim, and with great ease, that reality is true. Similarly, the notion itself of reality, even more so than that of fiction, is also malleable and polyvalent. How, then, are we able to separate reality from fiction with such ease? And, most importantly, how do we determine what is real in the past from what is not?

The past can only be known in the present and only exists in the present of the person who remembers it. The past is inevitably linked to people, to language, to its narration, and to the understanding of the person who reclaims it, whether through memory, or through the objects that come from it. The shape and place of past objects, in the past and in the present, are dependent on the interpretation of those who come into contact with them; The past is, therefore, a kind of personal and collective invention, which may vanish out of convenience, or due to circumstance, subjectivity, changes in habit and language, imprecisions, and all other kinds of difficulties.

The past is a kind of waking dream, a backwards future in which hypotheses seem more verisimilar because of their burden of proof and testimony. But the past will always contain fiction, and there is no clear way to separate invention from fact. Not even a photo of the past is free of fictional content.

What is there to say, then, of the present? How do we separate the perception of what we call "reality" from the imaginary limitations of the person who perceives it? Is there a communal and tacit agreement about what is happening, which in turn determines what is actually happening, and what is real? And, to what point is this consensus verifiable and how do we verify it, if at all possible? But it isn't possible. Consensus is simply superficial or, more accurately, it is beholden to sense and to convention. It is a superficial, yet necessary, agreement that permits everyone (or almost everyone) to share certain common limitations, such as the hours of the day, the setting, colors, smells, sounds, weather, and everyday communication. Without this agreement, life in society would be impossible.

However, beyond this, how do we establish what each person considers to be real? How many misunderstandings occur daily because of the different perceptions of what has been said, seen, or heard? How many people see completely different and sometimes even contradictory things, under the exact same spatial and temporal conditions? Of course, the notion of reality is ample enough to hold multiple, almost infinite interpretations of what is real. If, in the day-to-day, one person sees people, another sees trees, another sees numbers, and another sees bricks and pillars, all of these are real. This is not problematic, nor is it cause for doubt. But how many variations exist in these perceptions, and how many, and which, of these are charged with personal or subjective needs, with unique experiences? How many of these are exclusive to the present and have not yet become memory or, in other words, the past?

A person's need to separate reality from fiction is attributed more often to weakness than it is to clarity. The introduction of fiction into reality, and the acceptance of their inseparability, disturbs the limits each person establishes for themselves, both for those who insist in banishing fiction, like her mother, and for those who insist in banishing reality, like her daughter. If the daughter is so bothered by the fact that there is a consensus in venerating reality as truth and fiction as a lie, it is because, in some way, she accepts this separation.

The truth is that because her mother accurately experienced something that was undeniably real, she cannot bear the sudden intrusion of the unexpected into her expertly constructed day-to-day, and therefore rejects these as fiction. And because the daughter has a mother who experienced this truth, because she did not experience it herself, and only has at her disposal partial facts—which exist in the past and are only known by someone who would prefer to forget than to remember them—because of all this, she has to fictionalize everything she lives, and ultimately rejects the limits of reality as oppressive impertinences. But, luckily, nothing is that easy or clear-cut.

There is a dimension to the experience of suffering that is not susceptible to invention and narrative construction. It is what it is, was what it was, and was what it is. There is no way of learning the immanent "thingness" of a thing that has no edges, no buts, and no gaps. There is no greater way to be-in-oneself than through the exertion of extreme physical pain on one person by another. The unjustifiable, the absurd, the radical, the *sans* nothing, the empty emptiness. How can we inhabit this pain, once the pain is over, once life has "moved on"? How do we locate it in ourselves?

The other may leave, die, or disappear, but the pain continues. The other leaves the pain to the person who lived it; it is nameless and placeless, and cannot become history. Whoever hears the stone falls silent. It can be carried around, but it's impossible to turn it into anything else.

The possibility that there are things that exist that cannot be told—by anyone—also frightens the daughter. There is a way of narrating beauty, the infinite, and the unknown, that is sublime. But narrating horror in this way seems to sin on principle. So how do we do it? Perhaps only as Beckett and Celan did, by invading language and structurally breaking it, so that no trace is left of semantics and syntax, which subordinate everything to successive, causal understanding. In this register, the narration of fact is always a failed and mediocre attempt to give a name and body to nothingness.

Mother, if you were never really interested in writing, why did you want to write that diary, in Stockholm?

To show it to you!

Her response reveals again how much she trusts in the wisdom of fate. It is as if she had known, as if her daughter had been born to read the diary and share it; and maybe this is why she wrote it, even though she wasn't in the habit of writing. Not a single person she knew then wrote like she did.

Every person knits a narrative beneath and within themselves so that the threads persist and crisscross, able to carry on and to develop into other stories. In a way, her diary existed, in silence, even before she'd mentioned it, even when no one knew of its existence. Before she spoke of it, not a single person knew, or could know, where it was located in her life. Her daughter also can't remember when she first heard of the diary; whether it was or wasn't part of her childhood. Her sisters do not remember, either. So why did she, the youngest daughter, a teenager, feel such sudden curiosity about the diary?

It was her therapist who, in the mid-nineties, thought to turn the diary into a book. She claimed that the translation of her mother's diary would symbolize the conclusion of her daughter's therapy. She saw in this the daughter's appropriation of her own memory and her parents', of making these into an object, or, in the language of psychoanalysis, turning them into a concrete elaboration of her history. It was to be a kind of cure. The daughter commissioned a translation, her psychoanalyst wrote an introduction, and the book was sent to Moacyr Scliar in Rio Grande do Sul, who quickly agreed to write a preface. The project was presented to a publisher who, after some time, suggested publishing it as a young adult book. There was a competition between two editors at the same house, each of them pitching a different war diary. Her mother's was one of them, but it was the other diary that ended up winning. And then, in the 2000s, for reasons the daughter can no longer quite recall, her desire to publish the story resurfaced. The daughter's own daughter is also a writer, and she had the idea that they should both go to Auschwitz, to visit some of the places their mother, and grandmother, had traveled to—to see her story from up close.

Little by little, the daughter begins to understand and to agree.

Yes, her mother had written this diary so that she could show it to her, her daughter. It is not that it was her mission to do so or her life's purpose; it was not an unavoidable necessity or even a debt she felt toward her own mother. It was a coincidental coming together of desires and languages which somehow corresponded: the daughter's interest in writing and memory and the fact that she was the youngest daughter and therefore had greater access to her parents' stories, who by that time were in a better place to share their stories with her than they had been with the other daughters.

Her mother can't wait to see the finished book and even has thoughts about the title, which she shares with her daughter. Like *1944.* Her impression must be that the daughter is telling her story in a better-written, more structured way than she ever could. How should she explain to her mother that this isn't what she's doing? What will her mother's reaction be when she sees that the book is a handful of fragments, of diversions, of scattered memories, and of tattered attempts at interpretation mixed with memories that are pieced together?

INVENTED HISTORIES

When the daughter was in Auschwitz, she jotted down some of the names and addresses on the suitcases that were scattered behind the display glass.

In 2011, she searched for two of these names on Google: Zlenka Fantl, resident of Podenstrasse 22, in Vienna, and Raphaela Sata Tansik, of Blumauergrass II. There is no record of either. The streets, Podenstrasse and Blumauergrass also cannot be located on Google. It's possible the daughter wrote the names of the streets down incorrectly or that the streets were destroyed.

Written on almost every suitcase in Auschwitz is the owner's address, as well as their date of birth and departure; maybe this is an indication that they had in some way foreseen the risk of death, and that they also, by writing their names and addresses, hoped they would be found, or remembered.

What was it like for Zlenka Fantl and Raphaela Sata Tansik to write their names on the suitcase? How were they able to get hold of a pen? Did their hands tremble as they wrote, or were they steady? Did they ask someone else to write for them? Did they write their names beforehand, having been warned of the arrival of the Germans? How would it have felt for these two Viennese women to speak the same languages of the officers who imprisoned them?

What must it be like to disappear without leaving a trace, no more than a name and an address scrawled on a suitcase now on display at the Auschwitz Museum?

Zlenka Fantl and Raphaela Sata Tansik did not know each other personally, but their paths had sometimes crossed as they walked to the tram, which Raphaela took every Tuesday and Thursday, and was located next to Zlenka's granddaughter's house, where Zlenka visited regularly. Raphaela was from a modern family in Vienna, who were cultured and proud of the comportment of the city's intellectual bourgeoisie. Her father was a medical psychiatrist; he had studied and supported Dr. Freud's theories, with whom he'd sometimes correspond. Her mother was a reasonably well-known piano teacher and, though her own career as a soloist had not come to fruition, she had been content to accept the task of stimulating new talent in her own home. Raphaela was an only child and she'd been raised without mollycoddling or hysterics. She was serious and cordial, and engaged with certain feminist ideals more energetically than her mother, whose greatest feminist act was to pass her own maiden name, Sata, onto her daughter. They were the only Jewish family with this name, and both mother and daughter liked its singularity. Her first name, Raphaela, was also not traditionally Jewish, and seemed to hint at an Italian heritage rather than Hungarian or Slavic, which is where her grandparents were from. At the age of nineteen, she studied physiotherapy at the university, took singing lessons at night, and dated a Viennese boy with no Jewish heritage. This had been cause for serious conflict with the leadership of the resistance, which had, since the end of 1938, been pressuring the Jews in Vienna to unite around the same anti-national socialist cause since the end of 1938. Even though antisemitism was spreading ever more swiftly and incisively through Viennese society, Raphaela and her parents' friends were enlightened enough not to let themselves be seduced by this antisemitic fanaticism, and Raphaela did not feel that the atmosphere was as disastrous as some of her relatives and clandestine newspapers insisted. She felt a certain disdain for her frightened relatives and listened to Hitler's speeches with total apathy. On July 16, 1942, Raphaela heard that her parents would be deported to a work camp in Poland. Father, mother, and daughter sat in silence in the drawing room with the piano between them. For over half an hour, no one spoke. Except for Raphaela who, after scrutinizing each corner of a painting of a dense forest that hung over the hutch for what seemed to be the first time in her life, had asked: *Don't you think that tree is strangely disproportionate?* And with this they somehow all understood that there would be no coming home.

No, it wasn't like that at all. Raphaela Sata Tansik and Zlenka Fantl never met. Raphaela was from a modern family, and was young when she was taken away. Zlenka was much older and, because of her age, was killed as soon as she arrived at the camp. Raphaela was eighteen years old in 1943 when the Nazis took a convoy of Viennese prisoners to Auschwitz. She was beautiful—long neck, well-defined clavicle, and a sprinkle of freckles on her white skin, which was covered in strawberry hairs the same blond of her long, straight hair. Her eyes were green and melancholy, but held the shadow of a distant joy, as if laughter were always hesitatingly threatening to bubble out. No one who gazed deeply into her eyes could determine whether the tears that pooled there were from pain or excitement. In any case, she did not cry. She was discreet and quietly courageous. She thought of the food and the little luggage she'd carry on her trip, of how she would protect her rheumatic mother, and of the pen she'd use to mark her suitcase. At the same time, she pictured the overcrowded train carriage, and once on it, glimpsed the crop fields through the cracks in the door and asked herself what that strange bird, a species she had never seen before, could possibly be doing there. It was this peculiar polarity that had made Claudius fall in love with her. He feared they would soon come to take her, and begged her to flee. She agreed, but in the end never left, nor explained why. As if some absurd force was making her to stay. Perhaps she was simply certain there was no way out, or that it was necessary to live through what she had imagined they were going to live through. She could never have thought that what eventually happened would bear no resemblance at all to what she had pictured. If she had, she would never have given herself the luxury of thinking she was capable of tolerating it. And yet, Raphaela survived in the camp for seven months, after losing both her father and mother. She died, slowly, until the moment her death was finally consummated. It was, in truth, a victorious sort of death. To not let herself be killed, but to die despite the Nazis' murderous desires. There are many possible victories. Sometimes even defeat. Raphaela left her fingerprints all over the room just days before she died. She dirtied her fingers with earth and smeared her prints on the beds, the floor, the bricks, on the prisoners' suitcases—everywhere. The next day, the prisoners had to clean her prints off, disinfecting them with alcohol while the barrack's *kapo* yelled at them, infernally. But a single print remained. The fingerprint on Raphaela's spoon, which was picked up by Zlenka who, in reality, had never met her, but having found her spoon, had taken possession of it, and of her fingerprint. She used the spoon until 1945, when she died, but was able to forever protect this anonymous print. In some hidden place of her memory and her simple personality, Zlenka knew she could not destroy the only trace of Raphaela there was left.

Of course this never happened. Zlenka really did keep Raphaela's spoon, but not her fingerprints. She used the spoon as if it had always been hers and didn't care to know who it had belonged to before.

Zlenka survived her arrival at the camp, as if by miracle; she was older and no one over the age of forty made it past the first selection. Zlenka only lasted because she could sing, having demonstrated to the officers, from the very beginning, that she was a soprano. She did not know this would save her, but it's what kept her alive. She sang in the Auschwitz orchestra until 1945, just before the end of the war. Primo Levi and others have written about how every morning an orchestra made up only of Jewish musicians would play German songs to accompany the prisoner's march to work—just another of the thousands of innovative methods the Nazis devised to humiliate their prisoners. By making it sound as if things were fine, by forcing them to pretend there was room for music, and by twisting the music to such an extent it became odious. But Zlenka sang and, ironically, when she was singing, she executed her role well. Maybe it was because she couldn't help but entertain the fantasy that this might save her; maybe it was a flight of fancy, or vanity; maybe it was really just ridiculous, or that she had simply wanted to enjoy these moments with intensity. The fact is that none of this saved her and, as the end of the war drew nearer, the Nazis' most unmerciful practices ran rampant: Zlenka was killed as she sang, with a bullet through throat.

All that is left to tell here is that, at the moment Zlenka fell to the ground, dead, she was holding Raphaela's spoon.

No, coincidences are not so obtuse.

Zlenka had already lost Raphaela's spoon. Over a year and a half had passed since she had claimed the spoon for herself and, toward the end of the war, they were in overabundance. The Nazis were practically giving spoons away as gifts, and as many of them fled, there was silverware, clothing, and even paper and pens to spare. Zlenka did not keep Raphaela's spoon and the only coincidence that ties them together is that their two suitcases, which were on display in Auschwitz, stood near each other when the daughter walked by them in 2009. It may be the case—that is if the museum curates this display at all—that the order of the suitcases changes with some regularity and that, when she returns there, Raphaela's suitcase might be sitting next to that of Herman Pasternak, who was not from Vienna, but from Prague.

Herman was the third cousin of the writer, Boris Pasternak, who in his books never once mentioned the existence of his relative who died in the war. Boris won the Nobel Prize in 1958, fourteen years after his cousin's death, but was forced by the Soviet authorities to refuse the prize, which was considered an eminently bourgeois distinction. In a way, both cousins suffered kindred though physically distant brutalities. Herman was tortured and died in the gas chamber.

If Boris had informed himself about his cousin from Prague, perhaps he would have mentioned his name in his book, *Doctor Zhivago*, later adapted into a movie starring Omar Shariff.

Now did Boris Pasternak know Marie Kafka, who was also from Prague and whose suitcase was next to Herman Pasternak's in the Auschwitz museum. Marie, however, was not related to Franz, the writer of the same last name, who could have won the Nobel Prize—seeing as he was the 20th century's greatest writer—but did not. Franz Kafka died before the war began, which was good for him overall, because he probably would not even have survived the journey to a concentration camp.

Neither Kafka nor Boris Pasternak saw Raphaela's spoon or heard Zlenka sing. But perhaps Herman Pasternak did hear Zlenka, or perhaps he crossed paths with Raphaela. He may have even exchanged a few words with one of them. But they certainly never spoke of the coincidence of his surname being the same as Boris', or about Marie and Franz's surnames, because it wasn't of much interest to anyone in that time and place. Also, even though Zlenka was a soprano, she had never read a book.

COINCIDENCES

While the daughter wrote Zlenka Fantl's story, she spoke to an old friend of hers, who lives in Rio de Janeiro and is also Jewish, about the stories she was making up about Zlenka. She loved the name, and the mystery of her whereabouts and her address, and was enthusiastic about the story she had created. She knew that her friend would be able to understand the musical and poetic allure that the name Zlenka held for her, a name that recalls the collective grandmother of all the Jewish survivors' children and grandchildren; and of the surname Fantl, which immediately takes any Jew born in the Bom Retiro neighborhood in São Paulo back to their long-lost childhood on the corner of Prates and Três Rios, to the muted sign of the butcher shop where they sold the best pastrami in the neighborhood, which was sliced by Zlenka herself behind the old marble balcony in a small corridor where there stood a chair with a missing arm, which is where Zlenka's husband sat, a headstrong man with whom Zlenka was always bickering and who always, in response, simply shrugged his shoulders.

But not only did her friend fall in love with the name, as she had, she went even further; she discovered real facts about Zlenka, who was actually Zdenka. And she found that, just like Mother, this book's protagonist, Zdenka also escaped Auschwitz with the help of the Red Cross, traveling the same roads, and ending her journey in Sweden, where she also wrote a diary detailing her recent experiences. Zdenka, unlike her mother, however, stayed in Sweden, where she eventually became a well-known actress who enjoyed music, hence the coincidence between her and the character the daughter created, who was a soprano. There is a website about Zdenka Fantl, which references her autobiography and the atrocities she lived through, similar to those her mother had suffered.

The friend told the daughter about these findings and at first the daughter thought her friend had made them up, but she assured her that she would include them in her book nonetheless and was surprised by her creativity to do so. But in the end it turns out none of it had been made up. It was all true. The daughter and her friend were startled.

What can we make of these coincidences? Of all the thousands of suitcases on display in Auschwitz, the daughter chose one that belonged to a woman whose journey closely resembled her mother's. And, at the moment she decided to invent a story about her, she also somehow almost guessed at her connection to theater.

There are many possible explanations. That it is not exactly a coincidence; the daughter is dabbling in the kinds of sources whose facts are necessarily similar. Facts that, when manipulated, highlight the similarities between them. This is inevitable—and can happen to anyone—precisely because there are so many stories. It's possible that the daughter is also suggestible. Or perhaps it is simply a coincidence; a matter of contiguous facts. The daughter doesn't believe in fate, mystical explanations, or energy flow. But she's frightened. She doesn't want to be a mecca of coincidences, she doesn't want to hear of any more stories like her mother's. One is enough. Let other daughters bear the responsibility of the narratives, diaries, and atrocities of other mothers. Let the historical, social, and collective burden of this narrative not be excessive or symbolic, but simply the necessary and individual unburdening of a daughter and her mother. A daughter who wants nothing more than to remember, but also to forget what her mother has forgotten. She does not want to remember the stories of other survivors and does not want coincidences to crash down on her. But perhaps it isn't a coincidence?

What is a coincidence? Why are there sometimes simultaneous incidences? And why the word "incidence"? One of the definitions of "incidence" you can find in the dictionary is "a casual circumstance," or "the act or fact of falling upon, coming in contact with, or affecting in some way." It is a kind of cascading occurrence. And is the word "incidence" related in any way to "incisive"? No; one is an occurrence where the other relates to cutting, or to sharp or keen mental qualities. But an incident is also a slice in time—as they all are—that is, at the moment they come to be seen as such. An occurrence is only an incidence, or incident, if it is so for someone in a specific time and place and if it carries significance for that person. And a coincidence is two simultaneous and similar incidences that befall two different subjects who are ostensibly unrelated. What brings them close together is this similar incident. The probability of two similar incidents happening to two different people is very high, given that the quantity of things in existence is practically infinite. Everyone knows this. But the frequent beneficiary of coincidences must be one who is able to perceive these occurrences, slices, collapses, cascades, and assaults in almost everything they see. What one person might consider a coincidence will never be so to another who cannot see these breakdowns in day-to-day facts.

And the more coincidences happen to one person, the more she becomes a victim and seeker of coincidences. Coincidences happen to those who begin searching for them without meaning to. All you have to do is burrow under the day's skin to see as they begin to appear. There's no need to be frightened, either; the subject was searching for these assaults, for these temporal slices. The subject cannot stand the smoothness of time. He wants incisive incidents. He is a bit mad, which is what they once said about the daughter. "She's a bit crazy, or at least she acts like it," they said.

ORATION

Let the past not be layered like an onion. Let the women who baked while they awaited the arrival of the Nazis remain in the place and time in which they did just that, and let us not disturb them with our stubborn intrusion into their lives, already so saturated with facts. Do they need the women of the future to further overburden them? Let the women in the past continue writing their names on their suitcases with pens borrowed from the cobbler, from the neighbor, from the typographer. And let us, the women of today, remember them as we would a caress, without intruding on their chores or their sorrow. Let us keep with us the ink from their pens and the smell of the sweets as they baked, so that we can use them for our letters and our ovens without bringing these women back to life by doing so, without resurrecting anyone. Let us leave death, on her own, in the space she occupied. Let death not come from the past to frighten life in the present. Let the present inhale only the smoke of the past and let this air moisten it like sea breeze. Let our grandmothers be.

FORGETTING IS THE ONLY REVENGE
AND THE ONLY FORGIVENESS

Names: Tadeusz Jude, Roman Nadolski, Roman Yopala, Karl Kassler, Lao Rajner, Pola Fogilman, Sima Szfranska, Raquel Zucker, Michela Rayktop, Sara Pache, Lotte Neuman, Rita Mano.

A telegram recounting the death of rabbi Szmuel Kornitzer of Krakow.

A telegram recounting the escape of four Russians.

Hair brushes, shaving brushes, prostheses, glasses, buckets, pans, kettles, chamber pots, bowls, dishes, cookers, burners, plates, graters, thermos bottles, sieves, rolling pins, baby bottles, spoons, scales, measurers.

Two displays full of shoes.

Suitcases: Zlenka Fantl; Manski Alois, Wien, Podenstrass, 22; Margarete Glase, 14/08/1897; Marie Kafka, Prag, XII, 833; Herman Pasternak; Benjamin Lazarus; Raphaela Sata Tansik, II Blumaeurgrass.

HERE, THERE

Leda Cartum

TRANSLATED FROM THE BRAZILIAN PORTUGUESE
BY JULIA SANCHES

In February 2009, as my mother and I entered Auschwitz, I felt nothing. It's not that I felt indifferent toward it, just that I wasn't able to distinguish any emotions against the white backdrop of my life. I couldn't say, it's this; or, it's that. I didn't know how to say anything at all, as if all the words had completely dried out, and even though I tried to turn to one word or to another, none of them said anything. Nothing said anything and there was so much nothing accumulated in that liminal place barred from time that I felt I could barely breathe. I couldn't make myself stop to look at any of the buildings, at the historical records, at all the photographs, the names, and the shoes. I just didn't want to be there. I felt like I was faced with the opposite side of something that could never be turned over to reveal its original form, like a bell jar that held air so dense it was painful to breathe in or out. Nothing there seemed real, even though everything exuded a scent of reality I had never smelled before. Anxious to flee from there as quickly as possible, revolted by what I wasn't capable of feeling or should feel, and stunned by the realization that they had reconstructed a part of the gas chamber that had been destroyed by an American bomb, I drew away from all the buildings and all the exhibitions and dug my feet into the Auschwitz snow.

245

In her autobiography, Ruth Klüger writes of how she only become aware of the immeasurability of what she had experienced in Auschwitz when she was finally released. Looking out from the train, she saw how people continued to live their lives outside the camp irrespective of what was happening inside. Families still lived in their houses, they still sowed and still harvested, they still awoke every morning in their Polish beds, and drank coffee and greeted each other. At the same time, only a few miles away, she was a prisoner in a concentration camp. People slept and then woke up, they ate, went out, came home, opened the door, closed the door, dreamed.

This was when she realized that people had kept on living the lives they'd always lived; this was when she recognized the unbearable miracle of simultaneity: that things took place at the same time. The world has many spaces, each of them fulfilling a specific function for a person or people, who, at the same moment, occupy different spaces in which they live different lives. We are here, but our here is not the same here uttered by a person who is *there*; and as Ruth Klüger left Auschwitz, she had to face the *here* of others, and only then was she able to grasp the dimensions of the *here* that had filled the last few months of her life. This was the source of her indignation.

I often think of that passage and of the force it exerted on me, even greater because I read it in Poland, so near the place the author called *here*, though far from what she called *now*. Reading the passage, not long after I had left Auschwitz, I finally understood something else that had always haunted me and that revealed itself fully to me in that moment. Living, for me, had always been a matter of trying to understand this miracle of simultaneity. Since I was a child, this had always worried me greatly as I drifted off to sleep. How can I be in my room, lying on this bed with the light off while, at the same time, on the other side of the world, a baby is born and in the depths of the ocean whales sing and somewhere else, there is someone killing someone and another someone crying? It was almost impossible to fall asleep knowing that so many people and so many things were happening in so many different places that I didn't have access to—and all at the same time—while I tried to fall asleep.

But it was the trip to Germany and to Poland in 2009 that revealed to me the extent of my disquiet, that this simultaneity was not only spatial but also temporal. And it must have been this thought that provoked in me the senseless torment I felt in Auschwitz. To realize that while I was there, living my life, everything that had happened, which was or was not related in some way to my own existence, kept on occurring and echoing everywhere, as if the lives lived in other times continued and reverberated in our current lives. Those worries I felt as I drifted off to sleep showed themselves to be much deeper than I had ever realized. I was not only worrying about all the lives that were taking place while I was there, but also everything that had already happened and that somehow lived on within me.

It's difficult to gauge the size of my past and how fundamentally what happened before I was born has influenced the person I am today. The past is a shadow we gather; a shadow with no real weight, but under which our backs nonetheless still bow. If I am already tormented by the thought that I do not have access to the days that

I myself have lived, and which have therefore become no more than a memory, it is even more nerve-wracking to discover that there is a past prior to my birth that in some way determines the person I am. When I was in Auschwitz, it was as if I had gone to meet this time, an abstract time which nonetheless carries with it a concrete burden—little by little, I came to understand this—that at times felt stronger and more powerful than any tangible thing around me.

I was born in São Paulo, at the end of the 1980s. I always considered myself Jewish, though I never knew exactly why. Our family gathered every year for Pesach and Rosh Hashanah, where together we celebrated something that marked and defined our identity. I noticed this as a child, though I didn't know what it was. I had never had to bear a sign on my clothing that symbolized my belonging to a certain people. My life had always been exactly like the lives of the people around me, but I always knew there was something else that I couldn't quite put my finger on. It was difficult (and still is difficult) to understand the extent of the identity I bore, even though I always knew that it was somehow integral to me.

Being the granddaughter of a survivor means having an indirect relationship with the suffering that made my existence possible. There has always been an intermediary between me and this suffering, someone who had already blazed a trail through the sordid thicket of this trauma. I was born into a clearing, a plot of clean land, primed and well-kempt because my parents had already taken the care to pull out its weeds, till its soil, and sow. When I was a child, I would ask what the numbers tattooed on my grandmother's arm meant and she would tell me it was her phone number. But I knew there was something hidden beneath it all, and perhaps this is what has given me this perpetually questioning look, a look that seems to say, "What are you hiding?" This miracle of simultaneity is inside me, too. I have also always had an internal space I have not been able to reach—deep, vertical wells that I know exist and hold so much, but to which I very rarely have access. Stories that are a necessary part of who I am and how I behave, but that I remain unaware of.

It is like bearing a mark without that mark making any objective difference in the world. Judaism, which was a crime and near-death experience for both my grandparents, and an intrinsic part of my parents' identity, subsists in me, yet always at a remove in relation to everything else. It is no longer the mark of a people and it does not marginalize or exclude me. It is instead a presence that must be sustained so that its strength as an affirmation of my past and of my family, and therefore my own history, remains. It is a mark that has ceased to be determined by a reality that is external and that has become, to me, mostly internal and at times, even implicit. I research Judaism and Judaic history so that I can locate my own Judaism, wherever it may be; a Judaism that slips through my hands, even though it is clear from my physiognomy.

It's very hard to try to visualize war. All I can make out are vague, darkened scenes, a miscellany of images I once saw in movies, all of which were almost invariably black and white. Nothing here approximates what I'd call real. It's difficult to truly grasp these events that have so often been spoken about, and which, in fact, happened and had a concrete place in the world. It is even harder to realize that these people, who were there, in the middle of it all, were my own grandparents, my parents' parents. They witnessed the war, yet I don't know how to fully believe that it happened. I don't have the necessary tools for this belief, and so I repeat to myself, once and again, that I am a product of this war, that it was this war that brought me here, to the place where I was born and where I now live. I must always remain one step behind the present, so that I can conceive of something that I did not live, but which gave me life. Perhaps this is what the descendants of survivors are destined for: to recover something that cannot be recovered, to experience the constant feeling of pulling at a fishing line whose hook has caught nothing, even though it weighs so much. The clearer things seem, the less sense they make. My grandmother was in Auschwitz. My grandparents lost their mothers, their fathers, their families, their home.

Though it can be painful, watching war films can also feel like a relief to those of us who did not live through it. This thing that was once real is given the comforting shape of fiction through film, and so comes to feel external, as if the war shown in films modernized the real war and so, in a way, also negated it. A film about Auschwitz can help us understand the inconceivable suffering experienced by those who were there. At the same time, however, by moving this suffering to the realm of film, it also makes it more difficult to conceive of the possibility that real people, who are in a sense exactly like us, were there, then, and lived that experience. Often, as I try to visualize what my grandparents lived through, I try to imagine that it could have happened to me. If I had been born in another time, or if the time I was born in had been a certain way, different to what it is now, I would be in the same position my grandparents were in; it would be for me as it was for them, because I am in no way different to them. It is as if I had opened up a crack through which I could glimpse a small sample of the war, but though I stretch out my arms, I reach nothing. There's no use.

We are not complicit in the war and in the concentration camps because we were not there—because we came afterwards—but we are complicit in their memory. We all share the weight of what happened with those who were like us and through this complicity, we must be able to believe that the thing we find impossible to conceive of, happened.

What I search for as I look into the history of Judaism and of war, and into my own imagination, oftentimes arises from the tiniest details, somehow always unexpected, which draw out the beginning of a story. My grandmother's accent, for example, always caught my attention. The weighted way she spoke Portuguese, since I was a child, seemed to me to be prophesizing a secret, one that hid behind her clipped vowels and heavy consonants. These small signs sometime sprung up like the loose threads of a plot that from afar might seem almost uniform; loose threads that were part of a mystery I had previous knowledge of, yet was unable to reach. I would want then—and want now—to pull at these threads to see if I could find something that would better explain what I am, what we are; and yet I know they are only that, threads, and that if I begin to pull at them, the plot will reveal itself to be no more than an enormous knot, and I will understand then that it was always just that, a knot.

It is with this idea in mind—of pulling at the threads of an impossible plot—that I read my grandmother's diary. As I sat to read it, I wanted to recognize the nineteen-year-old girl who wrote down her most recent experiences. I would have to shift time and dismantle generations in search of the moment my grandmother sat down to write. Always this act of rescue, of searching our surroundings for something that will not return. Always this attachment to memory, as if there were something urgent we had to hold onto, to detain. As if the smallest act of carelessness might lead something of the greatest importance to escape us and therefore be lost to us. It cannot be lost, but remembered; we must hold onto this mysterious gesture which creates memory, especially the memories of what we have not lived but nonetheless bear. My grandmother, in her diary, really remembers because she, in reality, lived. She shares her memories with us, memories which are still fresh, and that are more real than anything we could ever write or remember. I must sit and read my grandmother's words. I must come to know these words which keep, each one of them, a truth we do not know—and yet one we touch, one we touch and feel nothing.

AUTHOR & TRANSLATOR BIOGRAPHIES

NOEMI JAFFE is an award-winning Brazilian writer whose literary career has exploded in the last several years, gaining critical acclaim and momentum worldwide, with her works being translated into nearly a dozen languages. After working as a teacher of Brazilian Literature for more than 20 years and concluding her academic career with a PhD on the poetry of Antonio Cicero, Jaffe published a poetry volume, her first publication, in 2005 at the age of 43. At that time, she was already working as a literary reviewer for the cultural supplement of daily *Folha de S. Paulo* and had published some books on literary theory. From then on, she started dedicating herself more and more to literature, working across several genres, including novels, short stories, essays, and creative nonfiction. Her debut novel, *The True History of the Alphabet* was published in 2012, and her most recent novel, *Irisz: The Orchids*, was nominated for the prestigious São Paulo Prize for Literature in 2016. Noemi also teaches creative writing in a school of her own, called Escrevedeira, and she keeps a blog in both Portuguese and English called *quando nada está acontecendo*.

JULIA SANCHES is Brazilian by birth but has lived in New York, Mexico City, Lausanne, Edinburgh, and Barcelona. She is a graduate of Comparative Literature and Literary Translation at UPF in Barcelona, and she completed her M.A. in Philosophy and English Literature at the University of Edinburgh in Scotland in 2010. Her most recent translation is *Now and at the Hour of Our Death* by Susana Moreira Marques (And Other Stories, 2015). She lives in New York City.

ELLEN ELIAS-BURSAĆ has been translating novels and non-fiction by Bosnian, Croatian, and Serbian writers for thirty years. A contributing editor to Asymptote Journal, she has taught at the Harvard Slavic Department and Tufts University and spent over six years at the ex-Yugoslav War Crimes Tribunal in The Hague as a translator/reviser in the English Translation Unit. Her translation of David Albahari's book of short stories *Words Are Something Else* was given an award by AATSEEL in 1998, and ALTA's National Translation Award was given to her translation of Albahari's novel *Götz and Meyer* in 2006. Her monograph *Translating Evidence and Interpreting Testimony at a War Crimes Tribunal: Working in a Tug-of-War* was given the Mary Zirin Prize in 2015. She lives in Boston.

Thank you all for your support. We do this for you, and could not do it without you.

DEEP VELLUM

DEAR READERS,

Deep Vellum Publishing is a 501c3 nonprofit literary arts organization founded in 2013 with the threefold mission to publish international literature in English translation; to foster the art and craft of translation; and to build a more vibrant book culture in Dallas and beyond. We seek out literary works of lasting cultural value that both build bridges with foreign cultures and expand our understanding of what literature is and what meaningful impact literature can have in our lives.

Operating as a nonprofit means that we rely on the generosity of tax-deductible donations from individual donors, cultural organizations, government institutions, and foundations to provide a of our operational budget in addition to book sales. Deep Vellum offers multiple donor levels, including the LIGA DE ORO and the LIGA DEL SIGLO. The generosity of donors at every level allows us to pursue an ambitious growth strategy to connect readers with the best works of literature and increase our understanding of the world. Donors at various levels receive customized benefits for their donations, including books and Deep Vellum merchandise, invitations to special events, and named recognition in each book and on our website.

We also rely on subscriptions from readers like you to provide an invaluable ongoing investment in Deep Vellum that demonstrates a commitment to our editorial vision and mission. Subscribers are the bedrock of our support as we grow the readership for these amazing works of literature from every corner of the world. The more subscribers we have, the more we can demonstrate to potential donors and bookstores alike the diverse support we receive and how we use it to grow our mission in ever-new, ever-innovative ways.

From our offices and event space in the historic cultural district of Deep Ellum in central Dallas, we organize and host literary programming such as author readings, translator workshops, creative writing classes, spoken word performances, and interdisciplinary arts events for writers, translators, and artists from across the world. Our goal is to enrich and connect the world through the power of the written and spoken word, and we have been recognized for our efforts by being named one of the "Five Small Presses Changing the Face of the Industry" by Flavorwire and honored as Dallas's Best Publisher by *D Magazine*.

If you would like to get involved with Deep Vellum as a donor, subscriber, or volunteer, please contact us at deepvellum.org. We would love to hear from you.

Thank you all. Enjoy reading.

Will Evans
Founder & Publisher
Deep Vellum Publishing

LIGA DE ORO ($5,000+)

Anonymous (2)

LIGA DEL SIGLO ($1,000+)

Allred Capital Management
Ben & Sharon Fountain
Judy Pollock
Life in Deep Ellum
Loretta Siciliano
Lori Feathers
Mark Perkins/SullivanPerkins
Mary Ann Thompson-Frenk
   & Joshua Frenk
Matthew Rittmayer
Meriwether Evans
Pixel and Texel
Nick Storch
Social Venture Partners Dallas
Stephen Bullock

DONORS

Adam Rekerdres	Ed Nawotka	Mary Cline
Alan Shockley	Rev. Elizabeth	Maynard Thomson
Amrit Dhir	& Neil Moseley	Michael Reklis
Anonymous	Ester & Matt Harrison	Mike Kaminsky
Andrew Yorke	Grace Kenney	Mokhtar Ramadan
Anthony Messenger	Greg McConeghy	Nikki & Dennis Gibson
Bob Appel	Jeff Waxman	Olga Kislova
Bob & Katherine Penn	JJ Italiano	Patrick Kukucka
Brandon Childress	Justin Childress	Richard Meyer
Brandon Kennedy	Kay Cattarulla	Steve Bullock
Caroline Casey	Kelly Falconer	Suejean Kim
Charles Dee Mitchell	Linda Nell Evans	Susan Carp
Charley Mitcherson	Lissa Dunlay	Susan Ernst
Cheryl Thompson	Marian Schwartz	Theater Jones
Christie Tull	& Reid Minot	Tim Perttula
Daniel J. Hale	Mark Haber	Tony Thomson

SUBSCRIBERS

Aldo Sanchez
Amber Appel
Amrit Dhir
Anita Tarar
Anonymous
Barbara Graettinger
Ben Fountain
Ben Nichols
Bill Fisher
Bob Appel
Bradford Pearson
Brandye Brown
Carol Cheshire
Charles Dee Mitchell
Chase Marcella
Cheryl Thompson
Chris Sweet
Christie Tull
Cory Howard
Courtney Marie
Courtney Sheedy
David Christensen
David Travis
David Weinberger
Dori Boone-Costantino
Ed Tallent
Elaine Corwin
Farley Houston
Frank Merlino
Ghassan Fergiani
Greg McConeghy

Gregory Seaman
Guilty Dave Bristow
Ines ter Horst
James Tierney
Jeanne Milazzo
Jennifer Marquart
Jeremy Hughes
Jessa Crispin
Jill Kelly
Joe Milazzo
Joel Garza
John Schmerein
John Winkelman
Jonathan Hope
Joshua Edwin
Julia Rigsby
Julie Janicke Muhsmann
Justin Childress
Karen Olsson
Kenneth McClain
Kimberly Alexander
Kristopher Phillips
Kurt Cumiskey
Lara Smith
Lissa Dunlay
Lytton Smith
Marcia Lynx Qualey
Margaret Terwey
Martha Gifford
Meaghan Corwin
Michael Elliott

Michael Filippone
Michael Holtmann
Michael Norton
Michael Wilson
Mies de Vries
Mike Kaminsky
Neal Chuang
Nhan Ho
Nick Oxford
Owen Rowe
Patrick Brown
Peter McCambridge
Rainer Schulte
Robert Keefe
Ryan Jones
Scot Roberts
Shelby Vincent
Stephanie Barr
Steven Kornajcik
Steven Norton
Susan Ernst
Tim Kindseth
Tim Looney
Todd Jailer
Todd Mostrog
Tom Bowden
Whitney Leader-Picone
Will Pepple
William Jarrell

AVAILABLE NOW FROM DEEP VELLUM

MICHÈLE AUDIN · *One Hundred Twenty-One Days*
translated by Christiana Hills · FRANCE

CARMEN BOULLOSA · *Texas: The Great Theft · Before*
translated by Samantha Schnee · translated by Peter Bush · MEXICO

LEILA S. CHUDORI · *Home*
translated by John H. McGlynn · INDONESIA

ALISA GANIEVA · *The Mountain and the Wall*
translated by Carol Apollonio · RUSSIA

ANNE GARRÉTA · *Sphinx*
translated by Emma Ramadan · FRANCE

JÓN GNARR · *The Indian · The Pirate*
translated by Lytton Smith· ICELAND

NOEMI JAFFE · *What are the Blind Men Dreaming?*
translated by Julia Sanches & Ellen Elias-Bursać · BRAZIL

JUNG YOUNG MOON · *Vaseline Buddha*
translated by Yewon Jung · SOUTH KOREA

FOUAD LAROUI · *The Curious Case of Dassoukine's Trousers*
translated by Emma Ramadan · MOROCCO

LINA MERUANE · *Seeing Red*
translated by Megan McDowell · CHILE

FISTON MWANZA MUJILA · *Tram 83*
translated by Roland Glasser · DEMOCRATIC REPUBLIC OF CONGO

ILJA LEONARD PFEIJFFER · *La Superba*
translated by Michele Hutchison · NETHERLANDS

RICARDO PIGLIA · *Target in the Night*
translated by Sergio Waisman · ARGENTINA

SERGIO PITOL · *The Art of Flight · The Journey*
translated by George Henson · MEXICO

MIKHAIL SHISHKIN · *Calligraphy Lesson: The Collected Stories*
translated by Marian Schwartz, Leo Shtutin,
Mariya Bashkatova, Sylvia Maizell · RUSSIA

SERHIY ZHADAN · *Voroshilovgrad*
translated by Reilly Costigan-Humes & Isaac Stackhouse Wheeler · UKRAINE

COMING SOON FROM DEEP VELLUM

BAE SUAH · *Recitation*
translated by Deborah Smith · SOUTH KOREA

CARMEN BOULLOSA · *Heavens on Earth*
translated by Shelby Vincent · MEXICO

ANANDA DEVI · *Eve Out of Her Ruins*
translated by Jeffrey Zuckerman · MAURITIUS

ANNE GARRÉTA · *Not One Day*
translated by Emma Ramadan · FRANCE

JÓN GNARR · *The Outlaw*
translated by Lytton Smith· ICELAND

CLAUDIA SALAZAR JIMÉNEZ · *Blood of the Dawn*
translated by Elizabeth Bryer · PERU

JOSEFINE KLOUGART · *Of Darkness*
translated by Martin Aitken · DENMARK

YANICK LAHENS · *Moonbath*
translated by Emily Gogolak · HAITI

SERGIO PITOL · *The Magician of Vienna*
translated by George Henson · MEXICO

EDUARDO RABASA · *A Zero-Sum Game*
translated by Christina MacSweeney · MEXICO

JUAN RULFO · *The Golden Cockerel & Other Writings*
translated by Douglas J. Weatherford · MEXICO

DEEP
VELLUM